The Enchanted Pillowcase

and Other Stories

Josephine
Cunnington
Edwards

TEACH Services, Inc.

P U B L I S H I N G

www.TEACHServices.com

Copyright © 2012 TEACH Services, Inc.
ISBN-13: 978-1-57258-317-7 (Paperback)
ISBN-13: 978-1-57258-821-9 (ePub)
ISBN-13: 978-1-57258-822-6 (Kindle)
Library of Congress Control Number:2005908689

Published by

TEACH Services, Inc.
P U B L I S H I N G
www.TEACHServices.com

Table of Contents

The Enchanted Pillowcase

African Tribal Terms Not Translated in the Text

Acimweni–brother

Akazi–women

Anamwali–maidens

Anyamata–boys

Azungu–white person (plural)

Bwalo–courtyard

Ca bwino–very well

Chikole–second payment of bride price

Chikoti–whip

Chinteche Boma, Chinteche is a village; Boma is government headquarters

Chiserakwete, ndithu–foolish one, indeed

Cipatala ca City Deep ciri kuti?– City Deep hospital, where is it?

Cipongwe–impudence

Dumbu–sister or brother

Dumbu, kumbi chipatala cenukhu?– Brother,where is the hospital?

Gogo–grandfather or grandmother

Halale – usually means the white settlements

Ine?—me?

Intombi–maidens (Zulu)

Khonde–porch

Mai–mother

Maiye! Maiye!–a cry of distress

Mhali, Cipatala ciri nkhu?–Brother, where is the hospital?

Mkazi–woman

Mkristu–a Christian

Molomba–watchman

Moni, moni, Mfumu! – Hello, hello, chief

Moni, moni, muli bwanji, lero?– Hello, or hello, how are you today?

Mpanda–girls' compound

Mphete–first payment of bride price

Mtwala–beer (Zulu)

Mwanga wood–a certain native tree

Mzungu–white person (singular)

Ndifuna kukwatirani–I want to marry you

Ndifuna nya Msumba–I want Msumba

Ndithu–truly

Ngaiwa–corn meal

Ngarga–lies

Njinga–bicycle

Nsima–porridge

Odini–come on

Sakuhona, nkosikazi–greetings, madam (Zulu)

Tata–father

Tixo–God (Xosa)

Umame–mother

Ziripo mphete–Here is the first payment

The Enchanted Pillowcase

Above the sound of the beating of drums the two little African girls could hear their father breathing. They had looked in at him a time or two and had seen little bloody bubbles on the corners of his mouth. His eyes were rolled back until only the white showed.

"*Tata*! *Tata*!" Mathilda cried, her face distorted with an agony she could hardly understand. This was *Tata*, and he was dying. Only a year ago their *Umame* died, and their home was broken. It was but a dear memory now to be taken out and caressed when things got too hard to bear any longer.

But the drums beat on. Rough knots of hard *mwanga wood* were thumped on cowhide stretched taut over hollow stumps. Poor Akim, only thirty years old, lay on a dirty mat by the hut door. Only a few feet away the tide of Lake Nyasa rolled on the beach in little foam flecked swirls that could barely be seen in the half-light. A big fire had been built to help drive away the evil spirits, and the old *Gogo* was already muttering angrily, wondering who had bewitched her son. In spite of drums, fires, and cries, the white horses of death found Akim up there in the heathen village by the bright waters of Lake Nyasa.

When he drew his last breath, pandemonium broke loose. Now, he could command these people no more. Everyone knew that back in his hut were boxes and boxes of lovely things he and his wife had brought from Johannesburg. There were all his wife's dresses and shoes, and tablecloths, "sheet beds," and "case pillows." There were blankets, dishes, kettles, knives, and sugar and salt. More things than these people hoped to own in all their lives. When they had tried to wheedle these things away from him in his lifetime, he had shaken his head and said, "No, these are all for the children. Lena would have it so." So the phonograph, the sewing machine, and the other treasures remained boxed and hidden. Akim did not allow anyone to touch anything. All were for Mathilda, Alice, and little Cameron.

But as the days went by, Akim began to realize what his sickness was.

It was tuberculosis, such as he had seen often in the City Deep Hospital in Johannesburg. Strong men from the Transkei, and the mountains of Basutoland, or from Matabeleland, would last only a short time in the mines. Then they would waste away until they were but bones covered with wrinkled black skin, and nearly every breath was a cough that brought bright blood. Akim, who had cared for many sick ones such as he, now had no one to care for him. The witch doctor brought medicine to cut into the flesh of his chest. But he would have none of it.

"That will not help me," he said weakly. "It is my lungs. It is far inside. Medicine in my skin is only foolishness."

The relatives had quite hated him for that, for didn't the whole tribe know from time immemorial that medicine cut into the chest helped such diseases? True, some died, but that was because the witch doctor hadn't cut deep enough, or the skins of the lizards had not been pulverized fine enough. It was all very simple.

It seemed to Mathilda and Alice, standing helplessly by, that those relatives could hardly wait until Akim was dead. They were standing-a voracious, greedy fringe of people all around the house, watching every breath and every paroxysm of the dying Akim.

"Is he dead yet?" one would ask.

"How long he holds on!" commented another.

Once when he cried out for water, Mathilda crept in with a little earthen bowl of it that she had scooped from the shallow cove of the lake. Tenderly she put her little skinny arm under his head to help him, but such a fit of coughing seized him just then that the water was spilled, and he got no good from it.

Then when his breathing became more irregular and more agonized, until at last his heart was still, the villagers, a screaming, fighting, snatching mob, swept into the hut right over his body. The terrified little girls heard boxes splintering, the tearing of cloth, and hard blows of flesh on flesh. Little Cameron awoke then and cried, but no one seemed to care. The excited natives emerged one by one with their hands full, and disappeared in the darkness. At last all was still.

Tremblingly, Mathilda lighted a little stub of a candle. Everything was gone. The boxes were torn to splinters. Papers were strewn everywhere. Weeping, the children clawed with little black fingers through the wreckage. *Umame*, down in Johannesburg before she died, was not like these people. She was a Christian, and buttoned the girls in starched little dresses every week and sent them off to Sunday school. She taught them little prayers too, in the Xosa language, so full of rhythmic clicks and unpronounceable sucking sounds that one's tongue tickled afterward. She had *given* them things rather than grabbing and stealing all that they had. The tears rained down their little cheeks as they realized their terrible loss. *Tata* was lying dead there on the mat. Someone had even snatched away the blanket that had covered him. Now, the things of *Umame* were gone—all gone forever. Suddenly, clawing around at the bottom of one of the boxes, Mathilda gave a glad little cry. One "case pillow" of *Umame* was left! There was still *one thing* left from lovely *Umame*! But it must be hidden, or they would get it. Then the little girl remembered that *Tata* had told her only yesterday where he had hidden his post office book. He had told her that the money in the post office was for her and Baby Cameron and little Alice. She must hide it. Shrewdly Mathilda did so. The pillowcase and the book were hidden as well as she could hide them. By day they were pushed up under the grass of the roof, and by night they were under her little body, for rats or white ants might eat them if the,, were left undisturbed.

*   *   *   *   *

Akim was only twenty when he decided to go to *Halale*. Up among the Tonga and Msisi people they were getting used to their young men going off to *Halale*. That meant they were going far, far away to the south whence their fathers had trekked long ago after the break with great black Chief Tchaka. They were told there was money in that legendary place for their sons.

There were mines, it was whispered, where Africans dug stuff for white men to decorate their bodies, or with which to make watches and clocks. They had to go very far below, and it was said that many died. They would go to *Halale*,, some of them, and leave wives and children, but they had never come back. Whether they died or settled down in that far-off place, no one ever knew. But others came back and brought the split bags for their legs, which they called trousers, and hard hides sewed up cleverly for the feet. There were the *Njinga*, which were two wheels, one in front of the other, on which they could ride as fast as the wind and not fall off very often.

So Akim was going. His whole family went with him over the hard, beaten trails, winding hither and thither, as far as the Vipya pass in the mountains. They walled loudly as he disappeared down the path leading to the south. Even after he was quite out of sight, they continued to bellow their admonitions after him.

"Come back, and bring us all some of those outlandish *Azungu* things, you

9

Akim," and "Don't forget," they had cried again and again.

Then they trudged back, already dreaming of the *njinga* that could carry a man as fast as a leopard could run and the matumba that covered up the flesh of their legs so the flies and ticks could not bite so hard.

But much to his family's disappointment and anger, Akirn did not come right home. He didn't even go into the mines to work, as others of their sons had done. They were disgusted. How long were they to wait now for the *njinga* and the sewn foot bags and the beads and the watch to tell the time to eat and to go to bed? For it was told to these people that time was the ruler of the white men. They had separated the day into times for this and that and the other thing. What foolishness. Everyone who had sense knew that there was no hurry about anything.

But Akim took many days to walk to far-off Blantyre. His feet were sore and blistered, and he had endured hunger and sickness and fear on the way. Then the train ride, in the rough native coach, along with the sweating of the people in the overcrowded compartment, made him physically ill. The lukewarm water in the little tank was soon exhausted. Intolerable thirst possessed him. Vermin bit him. He thought of the wide reaches of shoreland, with trees marching in a green procession down to the very beach. It was well-nigh unbearable. Yet the train lurched on, hurtling itself shrilly into the night.

After several vastly uncomfortable days, they drew into the outskirts of Johannesburg. To the country-bred Akim, marvel piled on marvel.

The rows upon rows of houses such as he had never seen before kept him speechless. Then the train came into sight of the great mine dumps, which looked like gigantic mountains. Huge black mine chimneys belched inky smoke. And there were people, people, people everywhere.

He hadn't realized there could be so many white people or so much grandeur in all the world. The noise was thunderous. It made him dizzy and sick to look or feel or listen. Again, his mind reverted to the long reaches of curving shore dappled by surging little breakers and the scraggled shade of the bush trees he had left far beyond the Vipya, where silence covered the world like a great blanket.

Someone had told him long before of the great hospitals kept for Africans in that great city. Hither Akim wended his steps as well as he could, though the activities bewildered him. Noise and tumult whirled and eddied about him. He was brushed and shoved and cursed, and yelled at for any move he made. At first lie tried to inquire his way politely, using his native Tonga tongue.

"*Dumbu, kumbi chipatala cenukhu?*"

People looked at him foolishly and went their way, leaving Akim still lost and afraid. He tried again, this time trying Citumbuka, his father's language.

"*Mbali, Cipatala ciri nkhu?*"

Still no one paid him any heed. The traffic roared on, with its scurrying and rushing humanity.

Now completely discouraged, Akim. tried once more. He seized an African man by the arm in desperation.

"*Acimweni*," he shouted in Cinyanja, in a voice much louder than was necessary. "*Cipatala ca City Deep ciri kuti?*" A wide smile spread over the features of the stranger. "A Nyasalander, I think," he answered in the same tongue Akim had used. "It is good to hear the Cinyanja again. Where are you from, *acimweni?*"

"Me, I am from the Chinteche district, up beyond the

Vipya. I am a Tonga," answered Akim. They fell into step together.

"I will show you City Deep Hospital," the stranger offered. "We are not far from there. Conic, we go this way. I work there myself."

In a few minutes Akim, by the aid of his newly found friend, found himself awaiting his turn in a large room with several dozen other African men and women who were looking for work. In spite of his odd, ill-assorted European clothes, Akim was a good-looking young man. He was tall and fine-featured, with deep burning eyes and an almost Egyptian cast to his features, as if beautiful Nefertiti were his grandmother. Presently he found himself in front of a desk. A sharp-featured white woman was taking data.

"What do *you* want," she asked, sharply. "Work, or a course?"

"Why, a *course*," Akim stammered bashfully, hardly knowing what a "course" was.

"Then go to that room and register," she directed, pointing toward another door. "Next."

Akim, to his joy, found himself registered in the "hospital assistant course." He was given clothing, and a native boy took him to the men's quarters.

"This is for those who have no wives," he said. Akim saw a long clean room with a row of plain iron beds.

"They have nice places for the married people too," the boy volunteered. "Good houses, with stoves and a stoop to sit on, and a little ground for a garden."

Akim considered.

"That is good," he said. Later, when he found out where his bed and his locker were to be, he went and fetched his things, stored them away, and pocketed the key.

"Keep your things locked up," they hold him at the desk. "Lots of sticky fingers around."

He fell into his schedule readily, and as his mind was keen and alert, he soon became a favorite. For one thing, even when he was back at his village he didn't drink beer or follow after dancing, as some did. Often when all of his companions were drinking themselves into a frenzy, he had gone off in his dugout, to fish in the lake. It was peaceful out there and he could think. Then, when a mission had opened a school several miles away, Akim had been one of the first to go to school. His eager, avid mind literally licked up every available scrap of learning. For a long time he was the only one in his village who could read and write.

That is the reason Akim, at the great hospital situated near the mines, did very well from the very first. He scrubbed, cleaned, changed beds, carried out wastes, and comforted sufferers who were fearful.

Akim was glad then that he had become *mkristu* at the Church of Scotland Mission. His hours were long and fearfully hard, but he had words of consolation in his heart for poor broken derelicts, shuddering with fear as death approached.

"I'm afraid—afraid," one would sob, tossing on the high bed. "I'm afraid of—death. What—happens then?"

Akim would take a moment then, when he could, trying to remember promises he'd heard the missionary repeat time and again to those in distress.

"Don't fear. God is there. He loves you." he would whisper, his hand cool and firm on a distraught brow. "God? who is—God?" out of maimed flesh minds groped for light.

"God is our Father in heaven, friend. He will watch over you when you are in the shadow of death."

Yet Akim, who had comforted many, had had no one to comfort him when *he* passed into the valley of the shadow! Or did he? *We* think that in his dark hour he had a greater splendor than human presence could bring, for even Mathilda remembers the ineffable joy that fluttered into his deep eyes a few moments before he closed them forever.

Finally, after a few months, he was put on emergency cases. It was hideous at first, and once he fainted when a victim of a mine accident was brought in so crushed and torn that it was a marvel that the poor creature was living at all. Whence came he? Would wife or mother and little children wait in vain for a loved one who would never come home any more?

Then, though he could never grow entirely insensible to the misery and horror, he fell into a most efficient routine, until he became rather outstanding in his small world for his dependability, his steadiness and coolness even under great stress and pressure.

He had been in the emergency work for about six months when a new nurse came onto the floor. She was a transferee from another ward, and was a tall, smooth-cheeked, brown maiden, neat as a pin in her crackling white uniform. Hither and thither she flitted, always busy, always smiling and gentle. Her name was Lena Mbombo.

One day, when they were getting their food, Akim noticed that her head came up to his shoulder. It thrilled him, but much as he wanted to get acquainted, tribal clannishness was strong, and he wasn't ready to get involved with any girl—yet. He'd remembered his mother shaking a misshapen old finger in his face and telling him imperiously, "Now, Akim, just you remember, you boy, that when you want *akazi* you come home. We will find you one, two, three of the Tonga *anamwali* who know your customs and your ways. You can marry here and have many sons!"

But looking at Lena, slim, lithe, and pretty, his taste for the Tonga girls was spoiled. They were fond of boring holes in their lips and putting in wooden disks till the upper lip flapped like a curtain when they were champing on mealies. Then they were contented with little cloth flaps hanging down "fore and aft" for dresses—not a quarter of a yard in all. How could he go back to that?

Thus thinking, Akim changed ideas more than he realized in those days. Down in the eating hall he saw that Lena was neat with her eating, using a knife and a fork as he had seen European women do. With a wry face, he remembered the dirty fingers and greasy mouths around a general eating pot in his own village. Johannesburg seemed very, very far from Nkata Bay these days!

Then one day while he was dressing a wound in the men's ward, she brought him a message from the doctor.

She looked down at a small paper she held in her smooth, brown hand.

"Are you Akim Msumba? she asked in a clear, sweet voice. Akim thought she pronounced Akim differently than anyone else had ever done. She looked up at him questioningly, and if she felt Justifiable admiration for his tall slenderness, she didn't show it in her lovely eyes, for Lena was all business, with no coy silliness about he.,.

"Yes," Akim replied. "Yes, I'm Akim."

13

"Doctor wants you in emergency. Accident case. I'm to go too."

So—now he could observe the busy brown fingers close at hand. He himself handled all of his tasks efficiently, fetching and carrying, tying the doctor's robe on, bringing this or that which was needed, always busy, happy, and smiling.

Lena noticed that he anticipated, rather than waited for, the doctor's orders. When a thing was called for it seemed that Akim had it at hand already. She saw he was quiet too, not given to babble and claptrap, and no one ever had to tell him to be still. He was courteous too, and obedient without groveling; maintaining a dignity that even the doctor appreciated.

Lena had been there several years; indeed, she had taken her nurses' training there, so she was a familiar figure to everyone.

"That Msumba's a fine young fellow," the doctor said to her once, when he had done some thoughtful thing. "Yes, sir," she had answered briefly, still busy at her work, leaving the impression that she had more important things to think about just then than any new medical orderly who might have come.

It was inevitable that Lena and Akim should be friends, for they were so much alike. This Akim, who went out in his boat up by the still magnitude of Lake Nyasa to keep away from the noise and frenzy of the beer dances, would hardly attend brawls he'd been told of in Springs or Sofiatown or other native locations. Other men would tell him of places where cheap beer could be found, and once or twice some of his acquaintances were caught and jailed in a police raid. But not Akim or Lena. He saw her sometimes with a book in her slender fingers. That inspired the young man to take some of his money and buy some books. If Lena wanted to improve *her* mind, what better thing could *he* do?

One Sunday night he was off duty, and he noted that Lena also had time off then. just while he was pondering this, she and several other nurses came down the wide hall, chattering happily. He stepped out and spoke to her.

"Lena," he said very softly, "would you go to church with me tonight?" She looked up at him, her face breaking into a glad smile. "Why, Akim, we were all just going! Come go with us! "

So Akim found himself one of a merry, laughing group. It was near Christmas, and it seemed that a children's program was being prepared. Lena was the leading light. He noted how she drilled and trained the little ones to take their parts in dialogs and to sing their little songs. She was so tender and soft spoken with them. This night she wore a maroon dress of some shiny cloth and her hair was swept back and held by little maroon combs. Again his mind

14

journeyed back to the primitive girls in his tribe. He didn't know even one girl who could sew a stitch. True, some could weave small loincloths out of harsh grasses, and dye them with juice of berries and insects. When he thought of the heathenism and ignorance, the filth and primitive superstitions of his village people, he thought he could not bear to do as his family had commanded him. He could never make one of those naked, ignorant maidens *his* wife. He wanted his children to be reared differently from the way he had been reared. If he had little girls, he wanted them to sew, and knit, and wear clothes as Lena did, not gaudy colors tied around the waist and head, but something with dignity.

He was sitting there on one of the benches, watching the rehearsal. Lena was kneeling now, adjusting a white robe on a tiny angel. She fitted the little gold paper crown, and arranged the children just as she wanted them—then standing back, in a high sweet voice she led them in singing. Every little brown face was turned adoringly in her direction.

> "Away in a manger, no crib for His bed,
> The little Lord Jesus laid down His wee head."

After a while she called Akim to help put up decorations. Someone brought in a tree, and all the young people came up to help trim it. Lena stood out as the queen of them all, or so Akim thought. Though the young man did not realize it, he was in love, and it was a new, delightful experience. For in his heathen tribe love played no part in marriage. The *nkhoswe*, or marriage planner, from the son's family would look about and choose who this one or that one advised would be a good wife to bear many children. Then he would seek out the *nkhoswe* of the girl's family, and *lobola* would be decided, or the "bride price." The two young people most concerned would not be consulted at all. What business was it of theirs? It was for

the old ones to decide about this marriage business. What could these silly ones know about such important things?

Now, strange thoughts invaded Akim's mind. Who could he find for *nkhoswe* in this big, booming city? And the *lobola*. How could he find that? Then Akim remembered that a distant tribesman kept a small place for selling used clothes near Springs. It was rumored even among his own friends that this man received stolen goods and kept them hidden back in a dirty old storeroom in boxes for months, till the trail had grown cold. Akim had been there several times and had been treated with great cordiality. He'd talk the matter over with him. But meanwhile, he saved every penny he could rake and scrape. His little savings in the post office grew.

15

One Sunday he took the tram out to see his friend, Gondwe, at Springs. There were crowds of black men and women everywhere, detribalized, wandering about on hard, asphalt streets and sidewalks. Some looked restless and lonely, but others were furtive and vicious. Dirty, brick metal-roofed huts in every state of dilapidation seemed to lean on one another's shoulders. There were people of every tribe—stately Pondo men; timid, wondering Xosa people; resentful Basutos; small, wiry Mashona men; and tall, proud Zulus. What a motley group. Some wore ragged, cast-off white men's gear; and others, blankets that scarcely swathed their gleaming nakedness. Then there were women, some of them in rather awful crumpled finery of bright yellows and red, who painted their mouths and faces till Akim turned away in disgust.

At Gondwe's shop they sat in the stuffy storeroom, which was not open, because it was Sunday. The used clothing hanging and lying about in every state of disrepair smelled of rats and tobacco and fetid body odors. Gondwe did not notice, for he was accustomed to smells of every condition and magnitude. Akim was so full of his errand that he was oblivious of them too.

For a long time they sat so, and talked. Gondwe's wife, a drab, flabby creature with sunken eyes and a long, thin black neck, brought tea on a tray covered by an incredibly dirty cloth.

Gondwe chose a cigarette, and offered Akim one, which he refused. "I will not start this business of burning up my money," he had said.

Gondwe only laughed.

"You are wise at that, friend," he said. "But look you. Are you sure you want to marry in this place? Why don't you wait and—"

"I have no stomach for the Tonga girls," Akim interrupted sharply. "What do they know? What can they do? How could I be happy or love such a one?"

"Love?" mused Gondwe. "Well, that's another thing again, You have been poisoned by white men's magic, Akim. You talking of that love this way. I guess there is no help for you, so I will see what I can see. You must be ready for paying *lobola*. Me, I can't help you very much, for I am a poor man."

Akim nodded, but he knew very well that Gondwe had many pounds in bank notes rolled up in his pocket that very minute. But he wanted none of Gondwe's money. Only his help in manipulating this affair, so lie could know whether this marriage could be.

"I'll let you know soon," Gondwe promised.

So Akim found his way back to the hospital, his heart strangely light, Someway he felt he'd accomplished something. toward achieving his heart's greatest desire.

About two weeks later Akim- met Lena down in the place of eating. She turned and smiled right at him till he thought his heart would burst. He edged nearer to her.

"Akim, what is this you have done?" her voice was choked with laughter. "You are living in Johannesburg, Akim, not in some native kraal far from civilization! Here they say somewhat to the girl herself before they are I spoken for.' The educated girls won't marry just any old thing these days!"

Akim's mouth dropped open.

"I should say something to you first, Lena?" he asked breathlessly. "Are you speaking truly?"

"Of course, silly," she laughed. "My people in Gumbu wrote me in great surprise that a young man here had wanted to *lobola me*. When I found out who he was, I was quite swept off my feet!"

This *was* a strange girl! Akim marveled at her speaking so frankly to him. Tonga or Nyanji girls shut up like clams and looked down at their feet all the time in the presence of young men. Not Lena, though. Her pretty brown face was bright and vivacious, and she looked up at Akim frankly.

"Akim, you know, I've refused no less than ten offers," she sparkled. "My parents say I am a witch, and they'll never eat my *lobola*. You were a bold one to write like that and never say a word to me. My family—they all are shouting now, telling me that I must marry in the Xosa tribe! "

"What did you tell them?" Akim looked down at her, literally trembling. "Have you answered that?"

Now Lena seemed abashed. She looked down at her feet much as do her Tonga or Nyanji sisters.

"Did you answer that letter?" Akim came a step closer, his eyes on Lena, who kept her eyes the other way.

"Yes," she whispered. "Yes, I answered."

It seemed as if no one else was in that room. Dishes banged, trays crashed, and talk babbled all about their ears, but Lena and Akim were all alone as far as they were concerned.

"What did you say, Lena?" The burning eyes of lovely Nefertiti seemed to look out of Akim's deep-set ones.

"I said-" she hesitated, "I said I'd marry for love and nothing else!"

"Did you, Lena? Did you say that? Could you love me, Lena? For I quite love you, *dumbu*! You're in my mind all day, till it seems I'm burning with the fever, and I dream about you at night. I did not know there was any girl like you. I didn't know what love was like!" Akim sat down beside Lena then, his whole soul in his eyes.

Just then the bell shrilled through the hall, and the busy workers knew they must go back to their work again. But Akim went to his tasks with a song in his young heart. Only a step this side of heathenism he, but he knew already that there were some things in this life beyond price and measure. He knew in his own big heart that no young man of his tribe had felt as he did about a marriage —in every other case someone else had made the arrangements; perhaps the young people had never met before,

Then in the weeks that followed, Akim and Lena found many precious times to talk. Once he went to see some of her relatives who had come into town from Barberton. They had brought a great basket full of food that Miriam, the cousin, had prepared. A large fat hen, roasted to brown crispy succulence was wrapped in a clean towel. Little mealie cakes, crusty and soft, were packed in a cracker tin. Then Akim tasted chocolate cake for the first time in his life.

They had eaten out on the veld beyond the city, and as Akim looked off toward humming, buzzing Johannesburg, all he saw was the mountainlike mine dumps. None of its misery and squalor, wealth and grandeur invaded here. It was so quiet, so peaceful, so restful. Though he little knew it at the time, Lena's relatives were "looking him over." They were sizing him up and watching his every move. For that Lena had lost her heart to this tall Tonga youth from far-off Nyasaland, they had no doubt. It was surprising to them, for she had turned up her saucy little brown nose at many good chances of marriage with high-class young men.

Miriam and Ben liked Akim from the first. His dignified bearing, his quiet courtesy, his sweet voice, and his neat appearance won their hearts. Actually they had come to labor with Lena and to urge her against what they believed to be an ill-considered friendship. The Mbombo family clan were not common riffraff natives, but were educated and refined and were regarded as leaders. They were clannish enough to resent anyone's dragging down the high standard of their family.

On the train going home Miriam and Ben talked for a long time about this. They had been sent with definite instructions to do all they could to open Lena's eyes to the danger she was in. Now, they too were in the meshes. No one knows from what remote forebears Akim had inherited a most extraordinary share of innate shrewdness and sweet wholesomeness of personality. It was so genuine and natural that Ben and Miriam easily fell a prey. It was they who had been approached by the indefatigable Gondwe on this matter of marriage and *lobola*. Now they knew the answer, and the very next day Miriam wrote the letter favoring the match.

Akim and Lena were married in the African Presbyterian church the next spring, April 17, 1924. She had a pretty white dress that she had made with her own busy fingers. It had been cold and rainy for a full week, but nothing blotted out the sunshine and the brightness in these two young people's hearts. Be happy then, you two brown-skinned children of Christ! For your happiness will be like the grass of the field—green and bright for a while, but soon to vanish. For we are all living in a world in which happiness is most transitory and ephemeral. We all need to learn the bitter lesson that eternal gladness awaits us-across the river, and beyond the sunset.

Akim looked down at Lena, quite filled with surging joy, at the trimness and sweetness of her. And she saw her new husband neatly dressed in a dark suit, and compared him mentally with the ragtag and bobtail floating aimlessly about the streets.

They had an auspicious start in their married life. Lena had saved money, and with it she bought a bed, a dresser, and some dishes and pots. Akim bought a sideboard for dishes, a table and chairs and a couch for their living room. They chose a pretty floral linoleum to cover the red cement floor.

The hospital let them have one of their houses erected for African married couples who worked in the institution. It was not long until they were settled happily in their new home. Together they cared for it in their hours off duty.

Akim hoed up a corner of the back yard and planted corn, though he called it *vingoma*, after the custom of his fathers. Lena, when she saw its bright spears of green peeping up from the soil, called it *immbila*, much to her tall husband's amusement. But when it was young and tender, and was dropped into boiling water, whether it was *immbila*, or *vingoma*, it tasted all the same.

Often, as they sat in the evening, eating from pretty flowered dishes on a neat, smooth, clean cloth, Akim wondered what pretty Lena, so clean and thrifty, would think of the dirty wattle-and-daub kitchen hut in his mother's kraal. What would she think of his mother, whose fantastic heathenish beliefs and practices appalled even him, who was used to them?

He thought of the marriageable *intombi*, one or more of whom his mother would have desired for him, clothed in a dirty loincloth. Lena's smooth arms and checks were different from those of the girls of his tribe.

To make themselves look beautiful and attractive to young men, they took sharp stones or broken glass and cut themselves in designs all over their bodies. Into these bleeding raw cuts on body and face, clay was rubbed to make the

19

scar dark and plainly visible. Many of them

sawed and filed at their front teeth until they were like shoe pegs, making a smile hideous to behold.

"*Eh!*" he'd heard his mother snort in derision, if some hapless girl quailed before the scarifying operations. "And you think any man will want to marry a snake? Stop your crying, hyena, and make yourself pretty for marriage." But Akim remembered that even as she had talked, her elongated upper lip, with its whittled *mlomba* plug, flapped angrily. And the aging scars on her withered old chest and sagging arms were anything but beautiful to Akim's opened eyes.

Often Akim had seen his wife doing a bit of sewing or embroidery in her rare moments of leisure. But he was not quite prepared for one surprise.

It was just a year since they had been married when Lena, a look of mystery and mischief in her dark eyes, told him to look into the second dresser drawer. Mystified, he complied. There, lying in neat piles were little dresses, gowns, bonnets, and bootees.

"See what I've been making, Akim?" Her eyes sparkled.

"Why—why, wh—?" He turned a startled face toward her.

"Yes, dear," she answered his unfinished question. "Our little one should be born in September."

Then the two of them thought that life could not hold more happiness than they had there in their little cottage. The mine wagon brought bread, coal, meat, *mpumpu* (as they called corn meal), sugar, salt, rice, and coffee every week. There was water to be had from a tap right in their own fenced-in yard. What more could they desire?

Again, as Akim thought over his good fortune in winning this precious Lena for his own, he thought of more superstitions on which he had been reared by a garrulous old heathen mother. Why, if Lena were up in his village now, she wouldn't be allowed to touch salt.

"Eh!" his mother would exclaim, her harsh strident voice shrill in her rage, "such as you would cause the death of all of us. Want you should bring death to the whole tribe and family, eh? Wait till your child is born before you touch the salt. We would all swell up like sick fish and die, if such a thing were to be!"

Akim and Lena's first child, a tiny girl, whom they named Mathilda, was born in the hospital on September 25, 1925. Akim had been born in a filthy mud kitchen hut, and hadn't known a thread of clothing until he was a big boy. He had been tied to his mother's back by a goatskin, the legs of which were twisted together in front. Lena wrapped her tiny girl in coarse blankets she had bought with their small salary, and embroidered. Akim had slept on a mud floor next to his mother at night. Mathilda had a little basket, and a coarse clean sheet with a tiny pillow for her small woolly head.

The years were kind to them. Now Mathilda had a sister of three and a half, Alice Princess, so named by Miriam, the cousin. Baby Cameron, a little laughing boy of six months seemed to be a carbon copy of his father. Akim had never gone back from *Halale* to his homeland. So his tribe and family had waited several years for the *azungu* things in vain. Why should he want to go back? Here were his wife, children, his home, and his work. What more could he desire than the things he had?

One harsh day, when the cold rain clung to the kitchen windowpanes, and the fire was welcome all day, *Umame* came home very sick. Akim had someone to take his work, and he took care of her as well as he could. To this day Mathilda remembers the harsh, tearing cough of *Umame* from the bedroom. The lights burned all night. Poor *Umame*! Little Tilda crept in once and touched her hand lying on the blanket. But it was so hot the little girl was frightened and crept back to her bed. Alice woke up then and began to cry. Like a little mother always, Mathilda strove to comfort her.

"Don't cry, sister," she said, patting the small clenched hand. "See, you'll trouble *Umame*. She is so sick. Father (lid not go to bed all night for giving her medicine."

"*Umame* sick?" the tiny girl questioned.

"Yes, little one. But see, Tilda will get into bed with you, and we will sleep. Then when we wake up, *Umame* will be we! I, and will be cooking some *mpumpu* for us for breakfast! "

So with the eternal faith of childhood the two little black girls went off to sleep, sure that *Umame* would be well and happy on the morrow. For what could life be like without blessed *Umame*? *Umame*, whose hands were soft and whose heart was warm. But God, whose ways are often hard to understand, did not will it so. *Umame* was no better when the sun arose that stark terrible winter day in 1930. *Umame* died that day of pneu*monia*, and left Akim with a bewildered broken heart, and with three tiny black children, like little rudderless boats on a stormy sea.

*   *   *   *   *

To the hospital, Lena's death meant the loss of an efficient and trusted nurse. But presently someone else took her place, and life went on. Her people in Gumbu and Barberton would miss her sparkling presence on rare occasions;

21

but gradually they became accustomed to her being gone. The church they attended would miss her activity and leadership for a long time. But time brought changes, until no one remained who remembered very much.

To Akim, with his three little ones, life became a maze in which he wandered, seldom finding any goal or satisfaction. The little house, formerly so clean and attractive, became a shambles. The busy hands that had kept order so deftly were still now, and Akim awkwardly tried out of hours to keep up the home. A slatternly, overgrown girl was prevailed upon for a small amount to watch the children while he was at work. Then Lena's neat petticoats and underthings began to disappear, so Akim dismissed her. But worse days were to come.

After struggling for six months, the young man got a deep cough and began to lose weight. His work became a burden to him. Then, because he was weak and sad and sick, he began to think of home. He thought of the swirls of surf spreading out in scallops along the beach, and the dugouts bobbing like shells on the waves. A resolve slowly formed in his fevered mind.

He would draw enough of his money from the post office and he'd go home until he could get well again. The children could run and play on the beach and eat fish and *nsima* and bananas while he was getting well. Then he could come back. In his illness he had forgotten the beer brawls, the malaria, and the dysentery that clawed the very life out of one's vitals.

After several years of clean living with his Lena, he didn't remember that in his tribe, nose mucus was highly favored for hand lotion, and that fetid body discharges were all around the village. He'd forgotten about pigs and flies and filth and nastiness. So, his clothing hanging on his wasted body like rags on a scarecrow, Akim went again to his village up beyond the Vipya. He didn't take the *njinga*, but he took Mathilda, starry-eyed and hopeful that her grandmother would fix again the broken home. With him went Alice and the baby, both too little to remember very much. Looking at their crumpled, half-washed little garments, Akim knew his Lena would weep and sigh her heart away if she could see their sorry plight. But he was helpless. He didn't know what to do.

The day before he left, Miriam came and begged him to let her have the children to take home with her to Barberton. But Akim, looking down at the little faces, eying him trustfully, hopefully, shook his head. These little ones were all he had left of his Lena. He could not give them up. Miriam went away weeping, for if they went up into that wild, unknown place, Lena's little ones would be lost forever. They would forget the Xosa songs about the great *Tixo* in the skies—indeed, their mother's language would disappear from their little tongues, and much of all she had taught them.

Akim had the promise from the hospital that when he returned, he could have his work again. So, little realizing he would never see Johannesburg again, he took his Journey northward. It was with the vain hope that he would find health of body and soul again among familiar scenes. But Akim, poor lad, did not remember the greed, the voraciousness, the utter absence of tenderness and devotion of his village home. And so, because he had forgotten in his sorrow and despair, he put his three little ones on Satan's choicest vantage ground.

"No, you can't have anything else," he had protested weakly, only the week after he came home. "I have brought you all presents. You have shoes. You have a shirt. You have a dish, and you have a headcloth." Akim pointed one by one around the circle of people surrounding his mat. "I am sick. I must save Lena's things for the girls and Cameron."

"But they are little, and like as not rats and ants will eat them before they can use them. Let us only look and see what you have in your boxes."

They begged and pleaded and threatened until, if Akim had not been so sick, he would have gone away.

"*Tata*! *Tata*!" the little girls cried. "Where are the trams and the stores? Must we eat with our fingers? Where are the spoons of *Umame*?"

"Sh! little ones!" Akim cautioned. "I dare not take them out or they will be stolen. Only eat this way a little while, and when I'm better, we will go back."

"But, *Tata*, this is not a good place," Mathilda whispered. "Yesterday *Gogo* got a knife and wanted to cut a hole in my lip like she has. When I cried, she hit me and said I could never catch a husband."

With that, Akim became quite angry and sent Alice to fetch the old *Gogo*, who was pounding mealies in the next hut. She came, a horrible old ogress with flabby, scarred skin, with only a loincloth around her withered flanks. She hardly looked human, much less feminine.

"*Mai*," Akim began, I do not want my little girls' faces or bodies cut in any way. This is my law, *Mai*, and it must be obeyed. Among the educated people this custom is hateful, and I cannot have it practiced on my children."

He was quire exhausted then and had to lie hack on the mat, and lie coughed for a long time. Tilda noticed chat when lie wiped his mouth the cloth was stained with blood. She had been roasting a bit of fish on a little fire of coals, as she had seen others do, so she found a clean leaf and brought him some, hoping in her little heart to help her daddy in some way. Poor Akim! He was nearly at the end of his road, and he knew it now. And the end came quicker because of the horrible worries that harassed him night and day as to what would become of his little ones. God help him! He had reason to worry. He was quite caught in the devil's trap. And he realized it. Then he began to call Tilda and Alice to him to pray. He prayed constantly as he lay there dying,' that God would find some way out for his babies. For no one knew better than he that this was no place to leave his children. Lena would not have wanted this terrible thing to happen.

And so Akim's last hours were almost a constant prayer, Mathilda remembers. The last day of his poor life he called her, and between tearing coughs, he told her that he had prayed, and now he had the peace of heart that someway God would provide a way of escape for them. He told her to be a good girl and never to let them cut her body or face or her sister's. Then he told her about the post office money, which was for them. He told her the last journey lie had made was to the *Chinteche Boma* to tell them never, never to let the relatives have the money he had saved for his little ones.

The next morning after Akim died there was a burial of sorts. A great deal of screeching and mourning and beating of breasts was resorted to, but those who mourned most were two little girls, the older one of whom lugged a dirty baby. Their shuddering sobs were hardly audible, but they sounded depths seldom felt by human beings. They saw poor *Tata* wrapped in a mat and buried in a hastily scooped out grave close to the surging waters he had loved. The beating of drums and the shrieks and screams were only a dream. *Tata* was dead. Now, who was there left to care for them?

Not an hour after Akim had been put under the sand, the children heard their phonograph playing in a distant hut, and saw their immensely fat aunt Nyamukalongo sally forth with an earthen pot to get water. One of *Umame*'s best tablecloths was wrapped around her huge body. Mathilda quite hated her, ever after that, and little Alice ran screaming, "The cloth of *Umame*! The cloth of *Umame*!" and beat on her aunt's huge flanks in futile wrath. She was cuffed and sent back to Mathilda, weeping.

When Nyamukalongo returned with the water, she came directly to their hut.

"There is *nsima* to eat in my kitchen there," she said in honeyed tones, which Mathilda distrusted. "You go and eat, and I will sweep your house. Those hyenas tore it up last night."

"You are a hyena too, then," Alice supplied, naively. "I saw you grabbing and fighting too."

"Me? Oh, no! I would not do such a thing. Run on now," and she shooed

24

them away.

Mathilda led little Cameron, and they went to eat. "She is going to hunt for the post office book," she whispered to Alice. "But I have it hidden, so she can't find it. It, and the casepillow of *Umame*."

Sure enough, in a few minutes the fat aunt appeared in the door.

"There is a small book like this I am needing," she told Mathilda. "It is a book your father told me to take care of. Did some of those foxes find it and take it? "

Mathilda just looked at Nyamuka longo without answering, and the latter took the look for stupidity. What she would have done had she known that the child had hidden the book, would not be difficult to imagine. Mathilda had felt her hard hand on more than one occasion, for Nyamukalongo had insane rages that bordered on madness. People ran for their lives when she was in a rage.

So when the children had finished eating, she took them back and they looked carefully everywhere among the shattered debris for the book.

"One of those other ones has taken it," she muttered angrily, and went away in a great rage. They heard shouting and shrill voices all the afternoon as she went from hut to hut, shouting and accusing. At one place there was a fight, for Nyamukalongo wanted to look into the "works" of the phonograph, and had gotten a stone to break the case, when she was stopped by the relative who had appropriated it as his prize possession.

"It is not in there with the spirits who sing," he had shouted derisively, proud of flaunting his superior knowledge. "See? Only the spirits are dancing, and there is no book inside! You are a fool and a baboon, Nyamukalongo!" Then the children heard blows and angry cries, and their aunt's shrill shrieks of denunciation.

The next day Nyamukalongo tied on the tablecloth, put one of Lena's pillowcases over her head, and journeyed by foot to the post office at Chinteche. Every movement of her huge, rippling body seemed bent on draining the last thing she could from the little orphans. She determined to tell the *mzungu* at the post office that the savings book was lost or stolen and that she, as the natural sister, was there to get her dead brother's money.

The *mzungu*, tall and serious, listened to her blabbing mouth for some minutes without speaking. Then he went and got a book, and ran down the page with his finger.

"Is your name Nyamukalongo?" he asked quietly.

"Yes, it is," she stammered, wondering by what magic this great one could have found her name.

"And your half brother was Akim Msumba?" the quiet voice pursued.

This was witchcraft indeed. The balloon of her amazing effrontery was almost punctured.

"Aye, Bwana," she answered quietly.

"Then, I cannot give you a penny. Your brother was in here two weeks ago. I remember now that he was a very, very sick man, and I wondered at the time how he could have made such a long journey on foot. He told me not to give you or any one of your family or tribe a single farthing, even if you got his book. The money is for the children."

The greedy woman could scarcely believe her ears.

"My brother told you *that*?" she panted in cold fury.

"Yes, and I'd be ashamed if I were you. He knew you'd bleed his children to death if you could. He walked all the way here, the picture of death itself, to get us to save the money for his children. He said he knew you'd take it if you could. Now, get out, and don't let me see your face any more."

For a while even Nyamukalongo was subdued. It was as if a cold hand from the grave had reached out and deterred her unholy activities. But not for long. She was soon on the warpath, fighting and as dominating as ever. The little orphans suffered much at her hands.

Another thing that Mathilda had hidden was her father's wallet. He had given it to her, and she kept it tied in her *nsaru* day and night; for the relatives had stolen every blanket and left them only this small cloth called a *nsaru* to wear in the daytime and to cover themselves with at night. They, who were used to bright, starched dresses and anklets and ribbons to match.

Someway they lived. They lived because they did not die. They suffered agonies with malaria and dysentery. They were so severely infected with hookworm that their ribs showed like tiny hoops. Stomach-ache bent them double. Ticks bit them and ulcers tormented them. Mathilda alone remembered *Umame* very well.

Then one day Nyamukalongo decreed, in her high, imperious way, that they were all to go to Blair's Village, some seventy miles up the lake, where the old grandma had gone. She needed Alice and Mathilda to pound mealies, to hoe, get wood, and draw water for tier.

Carefully Mathilda wrapped up the wallet, in which were *Tata's* twenty pounds sterling, the pillowcase, and the post office book. Then they started out. Part of the way they went by boat, always hearing their aunt's loud bickering and haggling over costs and prices till every encounter almost ended in a fight.

"Our *Umame* was not that way," Mathilda whispered to Alice. "She was pretty and clean and quiet and always wore shoes on her feet. When she went to bazaars, she paid the first price and went away.

"What is a bazaar?" queried little Alice.

"It is a big store where you can buy everything new and beautiful. *Umame* often went."

"What are you hyenas whispering about?" shouted Nyamukalongo, suspiciously.

"Only that sister has a stomach-ache," evaded Mathilda. Alice had learned to concur in these evasions, and many a beating they had avoided.

The *Gogo*'s village was not much different from the other one up the lake. A little smaller and a little meaner, perhaps. The food was not so varied. Beans were the inevitable *ndiwo*, whereas up the lake they had had fish every day. Nyamukalongo departed after a day or two, intent on furthering her own evil designs rather than to accede to the querulous demands of her willful old mother. The two were too much alike to get on well. After even one day, there had been loud quarrels. So the little girls were left with an ignorant and hideous old heathen woman. Their little brother was far, far up the lake. For the first time their little family were separated. It seemed that their darkest hour had struck. But God, whose ways are past finding out, had directed. Blair's Village, squat and mean, and dirty, was within hearing distance of the bells of Luwazi Mission.

"What is that?" cried Mathilda the first Sabbath she heard the bells ringing. Her arms ached from pounding the hard mealie grains into *ngaiwa* to make the stiff porridge, or *nsima*. The water had to be carried half a mile. The hands of both little girls were cut and blistered from the toil of the week.

"Oh, that!" sneered the old woman in answer. "That is bells calling fools to pray on Saturday. Others pray on Sunday. These *Azungu* are ones we must watch. They spoil all the native laws and customs. We must not heed their foolishness."

"I must go and see," declared Mathilda. "My work is all done." So off she trotted down the path in search of something to brighten the drabness of her days. Alice hadn't wanted to go, for mangoes were ripe and her mouth watered for some of the delicious golden fruit. She had found a tree back in the bush full of them.

The little girl was glowing and filled with enthusiasm when she returned.

"O Alice, I'm so sorry you didn't go! It was something like the church we used to go to in Johannesburg. The people were singing such pretty songs, and then there were stories, and after a while the missionary preached. I liked him.

He looked kind. I saw his wife, and she looked to be good too. She smiled at me."

"Yes," Alice said, "that may be, but some *Azungu* are always shouting and beating Africans. I'm afraid of them."

"Not this one, I am sure!" declared Mathilda. "I could tell. Next week you go with me and hear the music and songs and stories. I liked it, and you will too."

"I will go and see one time, but I don't think I will like it, for you know I don't like to sit still very well," Alice answered.

"You will like it," asserted Mathilda positively. "You'll see. You'll want to go again."

People do not realize that eternal destinies hang in the balance every day. We cannot tell, when we meet people, that it may be that some act of ours will weigh—will tip the scales one way or the other—for time or for eternity. That week how could Mrs. Davy have known that kind words she and her husband would speak would mean all the difference in the world to three little orphan children. The song they sang there that Sabbath was one poor Akim taught them before they left Johannesburg. It was made sacred to little hearts by hallowed memories. Both little girls cried when they heard it. It brought memories back too sweet to be borne of dear *Tata* and precious *Umame*.

> Ndize pafupa pa cinta
>> Ngano nazgonazgo kwa cinta
> Ndize pafupa ndize kufupiko
>> Ndize kufupiko kwa cinta.

Some people think that harsh words and cruel or unjust treatment toward children or people down in luck or poor may soon be forgotten, but this is not true. Wounds like these fester and mortify, and those who have said them will meet them again at the judgment bar of God. Jesus passed by no human soul as worthless. Even poor, untutored black people have feelings our Saviour would cherish. These two little girls were ragged, unkempt, and dirty. Yet Mrs. Davy saw in them something precious that she had traveled over land and sea to save.

Accordingly, the next Sabbath the two little girls put on their only garment—a ragged cloth hardly two yards in length—and trotted down the paths to the call of the Luwazi church bell. The church is built of bricks made and baked in a kiln right on the mission. The mortar between the bricks is mud. The roof is grass. The seats inside are bricks built up in tiers with mud for mortar. The floor is just the rough brick. But two little girls—two bereft, exploited, and extremely wistful children—pressed in among the others, eager to see and hear something different from what they were used to hearing in their drab mud village. The songs were so pretty, and the people sang them as if they were glad to sing. Then after a while someone took them by the hands and led them to the place for children. There a teacher gave the lesson study, and it was a story told in a lovely way.

"If we only had our dresses *Umame* made," Mathilda whispered. "Wouldn't these children be surprised?"

Alice nodded at that, for her little heart was still bitter and angry that everything they had should be stolen the night dear *Tata* died. And now they had to stay with and be little slaveys for the very ones who had stripped them of everything. It was hard to bear.

It would have been good for the little girls to "show off" a little then, for several of the children were naked, and many had not even a quarter of a yard of cloth in their clothing. Not one little girl had a dress; not one little boy had *kabadulos*, or trousers. just pieces of cloth, scant, ragged, and often so dirty that not a semblance of pattern or color was discernible. They would have been little princesses to be stared at and envied had they appeared in the frilled and ruffled dresses *Umame* made for them in Johannesburg. True, Mathilda had the money in *Tata*'s wallet, which she carried with her everywhere, night and day, but she dared not spend it, or her possession of it would be discovered.

After church they pressed out with the crowd. Had Mrs. Davy been too busy that day, or had she not been the discerning soul she is, Alice and Mathilda would be heathen women today, swallowed up in the frightful whirlpool of misery, evil, and superstition. But she wasn't too busy, and her kind eyes had been on the little girls all during the church service.

There, awaiting them on the *bwalo*, stood the missionary's wife.

"*Moni, moni*, mull, *bwanji, lero?*"

"Good morning, madam." (Was Mathilda just a little proud?) "We can speak English and Xosa. We come from Johannesburg."

Poor little girl, flaunting her little vestige of knowledge as a sop to her broken pride.

"You do! Why, that is lovely." Mrs. Davy was very kind. "Where are your father and mother?"

"Both of them are dead," Mathilda answered. "Our mother died in Johannesburg and our father died up by the lake."

"Aren't you in school?"

"Oh, no! Grandmother says we can never marry if we go to school, for no man likes an educated girl. She is too proud."

" But that is silly. Don't you believe it. Only ignorant people say that. You must come to school."

Then, to the two little girls, deprived of nearly everything, going to school seemed the most desirable thing in the world. They saw the little and big girls going all about, and acting as if they belonged there. If only they could do something besides pounding mealies, smearing cow dung on the floor, fetching wood or water.

Alice lifted her eyes to the good woman's face.

"I'm sure we cannot," she said. "I'm sure *Gogo* will refuse."

"Do not be so sure," the missionary said. "Remember, God lives, and He is stronger than your old *Gogo*."

The girls pondered this and talked about it a great deal as they walked home. They remembered *Tata*'s prayers. They little realized that the hour of their deliverance was drawing near.

That afternoon a messenger from the mission called Blair, the headman, to the mission house. Everyone was filled with wonder and excitement until he returned two hours later. He walked straight to *Gogo*'s hut. She was sitting outside, smoking a cigarette of her own making—tobacco leaves rolled up inside a pungent slow-burning leaf.

"*Moni, Gogo!*"

"*Moni, moni, Mfumu!*" The old hag smiled hideously. After a great deal of palaver Blair got down to the business in hand.

"There is a message from the *Azungu, Gogo*."

"*Azungu! Kodi!*"

"Yes. They want the two girls of Akim for school." With that the old woman became quite beside herself with rage. She got up and began to shout anathemas against all white people in general and against missionaries in particular.

"*Agaru, njoka, pusi, bongwe!*" she shrieked, as if calling them dogs, snakes, and different kinds of monkeys would wreak a particular sort of vengeance on these enemies.

"They will spoil them till no man will marry them, and then I can't eat their *lobola*! Who then would work in my garden? Who will carry my water and get wood and pound mealies and smear my floor? Who—"

"And they sent you this." Blair interrupted the hag in her stream of vituperations to hand her a package.

Curiously, she reached and clutched the packet. It was full of coarse salt, a very precious and hard-to-obtain commodity.

Strangely, her claptrap was silenced while she reveled in the little luxury, running her skinny claws into it and letting it flow through her fingers.

"This too the *mkazi* [missionary] sent you."

He gave her a small cloth bag.

Eagerly as a small child she untied the top and peered in. Then her face splintered into a smile. Sugar! a rare treat indeed. Only in sugar-cane time, or when someone found a bee tree, did the people even taste sweet things. Mrs. Davy knew the way to her greedy old heart.

"Well," she said, a bit truculently, "I'll let them go, at least for a week or two. But they can't stay in that compound for girls. They must come home arid sleep here."

"No, *Gogo*, you must let them sleep there, for, see, she has sent you good presents and is likely to send you more. Then the white ones can help them with their studies, and no one knows how much good will come of it."

"Well, then, but what about marriage?" the old woman demanded. "You know men don't like the *akazi* who go to schools. They spoil much money by wanting spoons to eat with, and soap, even sheet beds. Tsk, tsk, waste *ndithu*, Me, I never asked such foolishness of any of my three husbands."

"Well, *Gogo*, things are changing. You can get more *lobola* for girls who can sew and even do something with long pegs called 'knit.' They can make the long bags for the feet for them who wear the European shoes. Your *lobola* will be very big if these girls can learn that magic."

His clever words won her over.

So with many warnings, Mathilda and Alice were allowed to go to school. Once away, Mathilda took *Tata*'s wallet and went to an Indian store aid bought a blanket apiece for herself and Alice. She was shrewd too, and would not pay any outlandish price, but bought a new cloth apiece and some soap when the storekeeper named the right prices. *Gogo* need not know about them at all. That night, at the compound at Luwazi, she and Alice rolled up in soft new blankets and slept warmly for the first time since *Tata* died. The next morning Mrs. Davy herself took them to school. They felt happy and comfortable in her quiet, cheerful presence. A new era dawned for the little girls. They were happy again for the first time since *Umame* died, that terrible day in Johannesburg.

Mathilda's mind was very keen to remember, or else their birthdays would have been lost. For people in *Tata*'s tribe did not know or care about birthdays. Poor *Tata* had no idea as to the day or year of his birth. When questioned, the old *Gogo* was puzzled and vague. She told him it was the year when so many people died of the fever, and he was born when mealies were about as tall as a rat's tail is long.

Mathilda was proud to tell Mrs. Davy that her birthday was September 25, and Sister's was on January 7. Little brother Cameron's was on April 3.

"Oh, have you a brother?"

"Yes, Dona. He is up at the lake."

"You must Send and get him. He must have schooling too. Let's send a messenger to get him right away. We can't let him grow up in ignorance. Your mother would not have liked that, would she?"

"Oh, no, Dona!" Mathilda cried, tears standing in her eyes. "It would have killed *Umame*. It is lucky that she doesn't know what has happened to us since *Tata* died!"

Frequently through the years that rolled by gifts of sugar, salt, oil, bits of cloth, bottles, tin cans, seeds, and bread kept the old grandmother's demands down to a minimum. Alice and Mathilda were now about to finish all the schooling Luwazi could offer. Alice was a slim girl of fourteen, clever and astute with the "witchcraft" of sewing and knitting beautifully reposing in her slim brown fingers. Mathilda was sixteen, still sweet, responsible, and motherly, ever ready to correct, love, or do battle for her charges. Cameron was a long-legged boy of eleven, giving promise of being as tall as his father. All three had the proud Egyptian cast of features distinguishing them from the flat-nosed Negroid-featured people of surrounding tribes.

All three were leaders in their little world. Mathilda was a girl's "prefect"—a sort of *moni*tor, and assistant to the preceptress. Alice's handwork was the pride of her teacher, Mrs. Davy, who often had her up to her rambling mission house to help her. They were all clever, and absorbed culture and learning and little niceties as blotting paper absorbs ink.

Meanwhile Nyamukalongo was busy. Only recently Mathilda had slipped out of her greedy grasp and had gone five hundred miles south to Malamulo to school. Alice was getting ready to go soon. Nyamukalongo and the old grandmother had connived for a long time.

"See, that bad Mathilda has sneaked away for more education, Mal," she had pointed out to her wrinkled and wizened mother, enveloped in her clouds of tobacco smoke. "The *Azungu* missionary has stolen our rights."

The old woman grunted angrily, her old eyes glittering with hatred.

"Yes, and foolishness it is," she vouchsafed in her cracked, hoarse voice. "She's spoiled and ruined. She's no good any more."

"Now, there's that Alice," Nyamukalongo mused. "I've been talking in this village and that one all along the shore about her. There's the witchcraft of 'sew' and 'knit' in her fingers, so that her husband won't have to have the *kabadulos* made by them who sew. We can get the big *lobola* for her. I've questioned. One man will give seven cattle and five pounds for her for his third wife. Another says five cows and eight pounds. He has only one wife. Then there is an old one, his wife died a week ago, who will give ten pounds and ten cows. His daughter lives in the old village by the lake."

"That last one can tame her of her stubbornness," the old woman offered craftily. "He'll soon beat her into using the papaya leaves instead of soap and the grass strap instead of *Azungu* dresses."

So these two women drenched in superstition, greed, and heathenism plotted against Lena's sweet daughter, now happily packing her small possessions into her box, ready to go to Malamulo Mission. Poor child, a cloud darker than any that had ever hung over her small horizon now threatened to blot the joy out of her life. And Mathilda was not here to help her—Mathilda, who would take sticks, or stones, or her own hard small fists to protect her precious ones if the need arose.

It is the custom among these native tribes for the man to come to the girl he wishes to marry and ask her whether she likes him and will marry him. If she consents, he gives her a small piece of money, such as a sixpence or a shilling. This is called *mphete*. She can keep this herself.

Later, when he comes again to assure himself of her fidelity and willingness, he gives her a larger sum, such as five or ten shillings; this she is bound to turn over to her aunt or whoever is managing the matters concerning the marriage. This custom is important, for turning the second gift, or *chikole*, over to the aunt is a seal of the girl's willingness for matters to go on as the old ones decreed.

In the olden days few girls ever dreamed of rebelling against family arrangements concerning who or when they should marry. Custom, superstition, ignorance, and heathenism held them in bands of iron whence they could not extricate themselves.

So, one Sabbath afternoon a low-browed dirty fellow with a few straggling, discolored teeth, barefoot, dressed in hideously ragged clothes, approached, a little dubiously, the *mpanda*, or girls' compound at Luwazi.

Several girls were lying on a mat in the grass, talking.

"Oh, look! who's that?" one asked, watching the shabby old derelict shuffling near.

33

"That's a man from my aunt's village," Alice replied, peering in surprise at his black face. "Wonder what he wants."

"*Odi!*" He cleared his throat as he called out this customary greeting, asking for permission to come in.

"*Odini*," cried the girls in chorus, sitting up.

He shambled a little closer, fingering a disreputable old hat.

"*Ndifuna nya Msumba*," he mumbled, grinning a little foolishly.

"*Ine?*" Alice asked in astonishment that he should have singled her out. Slowly she got up. Perhaps this was a message from her aunt, for some reason. She was only fourteen; hence the idea of marriage, at least with a man forty or more years old, had not entered her head.

She arose and walked toward him slowly.

"*Ndifuna kukwatirani*," he said, grinning, as if telling her thus he would like to marry her would fill her with all kinds of maidenly ecstasy.

Alice's mouth opened in surprise. She looked him up and down, without saying a word. He was fumbling in the pocket of his dirty trousers. Presently, pawing and clawing, he fetched forth a sixpence and held it out to the still speechless girl.

"*Ziripo mphete*," he chortled gleefully, thinking that the pretty bird in the bush was already in his ugly hands.

"*No! Ayi! Iai!*" cried the girl, involuntarily saying no in the three languages with which she had become familiar. If she had expressed all the fear and negation aroused in her young heart, twenty languages would not have been sufficient.

It was his turn now to be amazed. Could it be possible that this little pig of a girl was actually *refusing him*, Bilwart Nyrendia? He gawked at her, scarcely able to believe his ears.

"Eh?" he said.

"I said, No! No! No!" Alice said sharply. "You're an old man-old enough to be my father! Anyway, I'm not old enough to get married! So go away. Don't talk any more.

"You're fourteen-plenty old enough for marriage," he said argumentatively.

"Go away-go away!" cried the girl. "I don't want to talk about it."

Chagrined, humiliated, he gave her one vindictive glance that boded no good for her, turned on his calloused old heels, and shuffled away toward his village.

The girls were sitting open-mouthed.

"Did you refuse *mphete*? Oh, what will your aunt say? She'll beat you,

Alice! " The sunshine had gone out of the day. They all sat in silence for a while. Then they went back to their houses.

$$* \qquad * \qquad * \qquad * \qquad *$$

Old Bilwart shuffled, mumbling and cursing under his breath, over the miles to his village. He had had no idea that the silly little hussy would refuse him. His pride was hurt immeasurably. He'd have her yet, and a few cracks with a rhino whip would take some of the *cipongwe* out of her. A man has to beat such cheek as that out of his *mkazi*. With Nyamukalongo's help he'd straighten the little whelp out in no time. He had planned on her doing tailoring work on the side to bring in money. Then with what snuff and tobacco her earnings could fetch him, his leisurely life stretched out long and pleasant before him. He could hire the little anyamata to hoe his garden, for little boys were willing to work a long time for a penny. Such delightful dreams hastened his steps; for he needed to enlist the aid of Nyamukalongo to bring it to pass; he'd even be willing to add a cow or two to the *lobola*.

Meanwhile the subject of the vicious scheme, which came direct from the lair of the devil himself, was sobbing on the sympathetic shoulder of Mother Davy, whose great heart has compassed and enfolded many a needy one. Alice was assured then and there that no one in all the villages could force such a hateful and unwanted marriage on this small brown maiden. Alice went away comforted. The power of the *Azungu* was great.

Nyamukalongo was outraged when Bilwart poured his grievances into her sharp ears.

"And she shamed me in front of the other *anamwali*," he groaned, as if the derision and laughter of the other brown maidens were harder to bear than her refusal.

"And that she-hyena refused *mphete*? She refused you?" shrieked Nyamukalongo. She stuck her fat neck out, fairly howling her epithets at the audacity of anyone who would try to thwart her. Suddenly resolution crept into her bulging eyes.

"*Ca bwino*, you Bilwart. Then you give me the *mphete*. I will bring her to time. She shall regret this. She is chiserakwete, *ndithu*. When she gets older we can beat this foolishness out of her silly hide. I will guarantee her to you. Give me the *mphete*, Be ready tomorrow with *chikole*, and in a week with *lobola*."

The sixpence exchanged hands, and Nyamukalongo sallied forth to the Indian's to buy some sugar and a few "store" cigarettes, which were sweeter than the homemade ones. A boy was dispatched to the compound to summon Alice to the village immediately, in no uncertain terms. She saw him coming, and hid. From where she was hiding behind a heap of grass, she heard the girls explaining.

"We can't find her. We think she has gone to the waterside."

"Well, then, tell her this. She is to come early in the morning to the village. Tell her it is the *chikole* business. Tell her if she doesn't come she may taste the *chikoti*." Even that small boy knew that a beating with a rhino whip was frightful indeed.

With that, Alice was seized with horrible fear. She knew then that Bilwart had paid *mphete* to someone and had received the formal consent to her marriage with him. She knew that *chikole* was to come after *mphete* had been paid and was really the first payment of *lobola*, or bride price. She knew that Nyamukalongo had received the *mphete*.

The next morning she hid again in the bush, sobbing and crying.

"I will fun away and let the leopards and the lions eat me before I will marry that baboon," she sobbed. "O *Umame* and *Tata*, why did you die, and leave it so hard for us? Why did you go away and leave us alone?" She was later to learn the answer to this question. She could later say with calmness and assurance that the God who took away, loved most tenderly, and that all the trials were necessary. She saw it was His providence that intervened in this crisis.

When the enraged messengers again arrived to take the child by force, she was nowhere to be found. With that, the Davys decided to send her immediately to Malamulo, to get her out of the clutches of her voracious relatives, who would willingly destroy her for gain to themselves. To soothe Bilwart, the wicked aunt presented him with *Umame*'s lovely chime clock, which had stood on their mantel in Johannesburg. He still has it, in his mud hut, battered and ruined—a relic of a lovely home that once was.

Nyamukalongo collected *lobola* five different times for Alice alone, only to be forced to return it, for the girl steadfastly refused to be coerced into marriages that were to her worse than death itself. Luckily, Alice was five hundred miles to the south, or she might have suffered bodily harm from the vengeful, wicked woman. For she was determined to "eat the *lobola*" of this clever, sweet girl, or punish her.

The girls' compound at Malamulo consists of a number of huts situated north of the church and school. It has a fence around it, and there is a long, rough class building called the Domestic Building and some queer little

36

kitchens for cooking food. The "stoves" are just three stones rolled close enough together to hold a pot up off the wood. All the equipment is simple and pitifully primitive.

There are three rooms in each hut. The room in the middle has a table in it. The room at one side holds the girls' boxes, and the "prefect" usually sleeps there. In the third room you can see several mats rolled and standing in the corner. The girls unroll these and sleep on them at night. Most of Africa's black people know nothing of innerspring mattresses. Here little Alice, Akim and Lena's girl, came gladly also. She was grateful for a mat, for a place on the mud floor, within these rough school halls—glad to work out her own life plan instead of submitting to the hateful destiny Nyamukalongo had willed for her. Here she was comparatively safe from her aunt's machinations. Under the thorough teaching of Dona Ruth Foote, Dona Ruth Higgins, Dona Agnes Vixie, and Dona Myrtle Pierce, Alice became a master at sewing, and was soon helping her black sisters who dropped stitches or awkwardly cut. out dresses. Mathilda carefully drew on the money in *Tata*'s wallet as they needed clothing, and the money, under her care, lasted several years. It meant all the difference in the world to the girls!

Then Mathilda was married, and Cameron was at Luwazi, so Alice was left quite alone. Again her life was threatened by a terrific temptation.

By this time she had been baptized and was rejoicing in the knowledge that the Saviour is coming soon. She learned to keep the Sabbath in her own simple way.

The girls have to go down to a stream nearby to bathe and to wash their clothes. Sometimes, in the dry months, it was hard to find places for either of these necessary chores. The water gets low and foul, and is covered with a nasty green scum. Someway, they get around these times of hardship, still thankful to be at Malamulo.

Then after they wash the clothes, they cannot plug an electric iron into a socket and smoothe them out. There are only huge, cumbersome irons with small hinged doors in the top, into which coals are put for heating them. But she was quite accustomed to such inconveniences and Alice ironed her poor dresses with these funny charcoal irons. Even though she did not have many clothes, she kept them scrupulously clean.

One day a letter was handed to the girl. It was addressed to her from Lilongwe, a small village nearly two hundred miles north of Malamulo. With genuine curiosity, the girl opened it. It was from a young man who worked as a clerk for a tobacco company. He enclosed his photograph. He seemed polished, smart, and worldly wise. He had a handsome, arrogant face, light in color, with no heavy Negroid features. Alice gazed at the picture as if she were bewitched. Never had she seen such a handsome young African man.

The letter flattered her ego. He told her he had seen her when she passed through Lilongwe in the opening of the school year, and that he had never seen such a beautiful African girl in all his life. He said her lovely face had been in his mind ever since, until such a great love sickness had seized him that he was unable to do his work properly. He signed himself her silent lover, Nedson Gombe.

The girl pondered. This man was no wrinkled old chief with several wives, nor a dilapidated, uncouth widower of uncertain age. This was a young man— good looking, educated, and established in good-paying work.

Then he told her he was coming to Malamulo to see her, and he named a date. It took so long for letters to travel that when the girl looked at the calendar, she saw that the time he was to come was that very day. Alice leaped to her feet and ran to her hut. Hurriedly she got soap and ran to the waterside. He might come any minute!

Then when she returned, she put on her best dress, an inexpensive yellow cotton print that she had made only recently. She didn't own shoes, or ribbons, or anklets to deck her small black person. But she did the best she could.

Then she began to worry about what the old ones would say if she had a man caller. Maybe they would refuse to let her see him! Poor child! She had become quite enamored of his picture. She had no one to tell her that she would be linking her young life with an enemy of God. She had not stopped to realize that this young man was a heathen. Lena would have told her and warned her. But now all the link left from dear *Umame* was a yellowed pillowcase, secretly stored away with her worn wallet in her box at the compound. She had not unfolded the square of cloth since the unhappy night *Tata* had died.

She dared not-nor did she want to-ask advice of the good teachers. Instinctively she knew what they would say. So the girl, decked out in her simple best, started walking up the mission road. Maybe she would meet him! What would she say?

Just then a car stopped in front of the African hospital, and a young African man got out. He had gotten a lift to Malamulo from an Indian.

Alice's heart was in her mouth. It was Gombe.

Slowly he turned around and recognized her,

By walking slowly along the road, they managed to talk enough to satisfy themselves, yet arouse no adverse comment.

"I've come with *mphete*," he said softly.

Her eyes lighted up, he noticed quickly.

"I've built a house, girl, and it is as the house of white people. You will not have to smear the cow dung on the floor like the other women. You need not spoil your little hands. There will be a boy hired to bring you wood and water and wash the clothes. Here, dear one. Take the *mphete*! I will come tomorrow with chikoli. Then I will go north and arrange *lobola* with Nyamukalongo—"

He held a shining half crown out to Alice.

"For tea money, precious one," he whispered. "Soon you'll be away from the tales of these dreadful missionaries of a soon-coming Lord and a burning hell! All lies, lies, *ngarga*! Ahead of you are cinemas, dances, laughter, cigarettes, joy, and sweet beer! Take the *mphete*, Alice, and seal our promise of love to each other!"

Involuntarily the girl put her hands behind her back. All, all came back. Nyamukalongo prancing and dancing with great galumphing grunts, till sweat ran in streams from her fat, black body. *Tata* sitting quietly on the *khonde*, sick and wasted and coughing, there with his little ones. All the time he was counseling between fits of coughing.

"Never, never do that, my little girls," he had said, "It is heathen-it is terrible, and leads to all kinds of badness. *Umame* would not want you to. You must grow up to be like your sweet *Umame*—"

There in the flickering twilight they had solemnly promised *Tata* that they would never dance and prance and drink vile beer, brewed in great pots covered with froth. And here was Nedson—handsome, desirable—offering the very things *Tata* had hated! She drew back from his clutching hands, his burning eyes.

"I will tell you tomorrow," she whispered hesitatingly.

"Why not today?" he asked softly, puzzled at her reluctance.

"Tomorrow," she insisted.

So they parted, he, to see an old friend at the Makwasa Tea Estate, she to the little *mpanda* hut.

She went to the room—mud floored, mud walled—that she shared with ten other girls. Their sleeping mats were stacked in a corner. She went directly to her box and drew out the yellowed pillowcase. One thing of *Umame*'s. Oh! if only *Umame* were here to tell her what to do. She spread out the yellowed length curiously. It had been tied up for years. It was one of those pillowcases Africans are so fond of making, with loving greetings embroidered on it in bright threads. It read:

"Happy New Year 1929"
"Lena Msumba from Miriam B. *Nkosi*, cousin
Transvaal   Barberton Hospital
Love to love"

The girl, reading it for the first time since she had grown up, was astonished. Here was a link with *Umame* that she had not realized she had. Here was a name. Here was an address. Then, sitting there, the spell of the insistent dark eyes swept over her again. She looked at the rough *mpanda* hut in distaste. A brick house—a proper bed—shoes—a watch. Well, neither *Umame* nor *Tata* could help her now; so she'd have to choose for herself. Not one farthing did she have to pay for school fees due very soon. Here was escape.

So Alice began to pack her belongings. She would go away with Gombe tomorrow and have done with all her worries. So does the devil deceive his poor victims. Peace, indeed, Alice? Nothing is before you but ruin and misery! Folding, smoothing her poor clothes, she put them into the rough kerosene box, her only trunk.

Just then a figure darkened the door of the hut. Alice looked up, wide-eyed. It was the dear Dona, whom she loved, who had only lately come from far-off America. Dona Edwards! She had not wanted her to know of her running away. She had not dared to think of *her*, for it was into this new Dona's hands that Mother Davy had committed the responsibility of this dusky little maiden.

Never a day had passed but this new Dona had greeted her kindly. One day she called her into her sitting room and gave her a pretty handkerchief. How the girl had treasured that dainty square of cambric! It made her a little proud too, for she was the only girl in the *mpanda* at Malamulo who owned one.

Now, of all times, why had this Dona come? She needed to hurry the packing if she was to leave at daybreak on the morrow. Warily she covered her half-packed box with a blanket.

"Did you want me, Dona?" Alice asked breathlessly.

The Dona's glance wandered over to the blanket-covered box—then back to the girl's face, covered once again with indecision.

"What are you doing, Alice?" Her glance was so kindly, so disarming, so friendly, that the girl was filled with misery. Could she deceive this Dona? What could she do? She began to tremble violently.

Then a white hand reached out and patted the brown shoulder. It was too much. Suddenly the girl burst into a flood of weeping and sobbing. She was on her knees in front of this dear Dona, her head was in her lap, and the loving hand of the white woman was patting the heaving shoulders.

"There, there, dear! do not cry so hard!" a soft voice said. "There must be a great burden on your poor heart or you would not be so troubled. Wouldn't you like to tell me, dear? Perhaps I can help you!"

As Alice sat there, her head in the lap of the Dona, the years seemed to slip back suddenly, and she was weeping over some childish trouble in loving *Umame*'s arms.

Comfort came to her heart. The dances and the beer, the strong sweat and the stamping bare feet, seemed again quite horrible,

"I don't want to go, Dona, now; I don't want to go"' she wailed afresh. "I want to stay——o-o-o-oh, what can I do, what can I do?"

"Go where, child? Go where?" Then with one sweep the Dona threw the blanket back off the box, revealing the pitiful little piles of things—rough, ragged, sleazy, faded—pitifully few. Her white sisters would say they were not fit for mop rags.

Then, bit by bit, the whole story was out. And the pillowcase, the yellowed treasure, was spread before this new Dona. She pondered a minute, then she spoke.

"I'll tell you what, Alice. You come up to me. There is a neat little room built for a servant's room up at my house. You can live there. Then, soon, we are going to South Africa. We will take you with us, and we can hunt for your dear mama's people in the Transvaal. You must obey your *Tata*. You must never see this young man again. God has someone for you, if you yield your heart to Him."

Slowly the sobs subsided. The girl Jay relaxed, her head yet on the Dona's lap. She lay almost basking under the rare pleasure of soft words full of promise and comfort and of caresses unknown through the long years since *Tata* and *Umame* had gone to their rest.

The girl carried her little belongings up to the big mission home. Here the clean little room was awaiting her. The Dona had gotten clean, strong sheets for her bed. There was a pillow too, the first real one she had had since *Umame*'s were taken away by Nyamukalongo. She and Mathilda had made some by stuffing little rough homemade bags with dry grass. There had never been money for anything better. There had not been money for soap, either, many, many times. Then the girls had crushed papaya leaves, which made a queer little lather, and they had used it as well as they could.

"I will work for you, Dona, all my life," the girl cried, when she looked at her room, sweet and inviting, before her. Yet it was all poor—very, very poor. The dresser was built of boxes; the bed was homemade; the curtains were coarse and patched. But it looked like heaven to a black girl who had for years slept on floors smeared with hardened cow dung, on mats woven from reeds.

There was much to do, for very soon Dona and Bwana Edwards had to go on their furlough to the coast. All the various and sundry things had to be packed in great boxes and the lids nailed up, just as if they were going to move. Dresses and slips needed to be made, and there was knitting to do. Then Alice had school every day, for she was taking standard seven, or equivalent to grade nine in other places. Every moment, every hour, was full.

When the pantry was being cleared, Alice and Dona Edwards saw to it that every fruit jar and bottle was packed full of something—tomatoes, pineapple, peaches, guavas, mulberries—just anything so that the bottles were not empty. When they came back in March, most of the fruits would be gone, and there would be many long weeks' even months, to wait before fruits would be available again. The last few days were filled with activity.

At last September 28, 1949, arrived. The car was packed, and a last look was taken at the address on that old yellow pillowcase—Miriam B. *Nkosi*, Barberton Hospital, Barberton, Transvaal.

A deep exhilaration filled the girl, for everyone wants to be proud of something of his own, and Alice had had nothing of her own father's people to look back on with any degree of joy or possession. There was Nyamukalongo, gross, greedy, and utterly heathen in every act and deed. There was her old *Gogo, Tata*'s mother, muttering and mumbling over her clay mug of *mtwala* beer, frothy and sour, and her tobacco and snuff, that rotted her teeth clear down to the gums. Her great upper lip had been stretched and pulled down and a disc inserted. It flapped like an old black curtain when she ate or talked. *Tata* had risen above such acts and such a life; yet he had died and left his little ones in the mire of heathenism. Only God had lifted them out. No, *Tata*'s people were not such as she could be proud of; all they cared for was collecting an opulent *lobola* and enriching themselves at her misery and servitude.

Through famine-striken Mozambique, suffering with drought, the new black Chevrolet wended its way. The people there, underfed and listless, moved like weary slugs about their dead gardens, burned fields, and tumbledown mud huts.

Then they were in Southern Rhodesia, wider awake, greener in places, with cities dotting the bright veld. It was a miraculous kaleidoscope to the young girl whose eyes had for years seen nothing but mud and dung, tangled bush and rocky hillsides, and sweeps of deep water swirling into foam.

At long last, after several days of leisurely travel, the beautiful little city of

Barberton lay before them like a mauve jewel in the green lap of the mountains. The jacaranda trees were such a riot of bloom that the city seemed caught in the meshes of a dainty lavender veil.

"Here," whispered Alice, her eyes bright as stars, "here is where the one lives who gave *Umame* the pillowcase. I hope she is here. I hope I can find someone who belonged to dear *Umame*."

Bright tears stood in her eyes. Then there was a sign with an arrow—

BARBERTON HOSPITAL

Soon the car drew up in front of a clean, rambling structure, surrounded by lovely lawns and blooming flowers. Alice and her Dona got out and went up the walk. A few inquiries led them to the scrupulously clean section reserved for African people. A nurse greeted them courteously.

"Do you have an African nurse here whose name is Miriam *Nkosi*?" asked the Dona. Alice held her breath, waiting for the answer.

The nurse smiled brightly.

"Oh, yes," she said warmly. "She is very good and faithful. We like Miriam very much."

"She is my cousin," ventured Alice shyly. The nurse darted an appreciative glance at the neat brown maiden.

"She is? Well, why don't you stay here and take the nurses' course? We are looking for girls like you."

Then without waiting for a reply, she led the two to a pretty green lane at the back of the building.

"Go that way," she said, "and you will come to the outpatients' section. There you will find Mrs. *Nkosi*. She has charge of the outpatients."

A little office stood in the midst of the cottages in which people who were able could camp and sleep while taking treatments.

A neat African woman clad in a crackling white uniform came to meet them. Her nurse's veil hung in filmy folds down to her shoulders, over her neatly smoothed hair.

"*Sakubona, nkosikazi*," her voice was mellow, and there was a look in the soft, lovely eyes that reminded one of Alice.

"Are you Miriam *Nkosi*?"

A look of wonder crossed the woman's face.

"Why, yes, madam," she replied in perfect English.

"Then I have brought you a cousin of yours. This is Alice Princess

Msumba." Alice stepped forward, her eyes on the woman's sweet face.

"Why, you look like *Umame!*" she cried in great wonder.

"Is this Lena and Akim's little girl?" exclaimed Miriam, taking the slim girl into her loving arms. Tears were coursing down her plump brown cheeks.

"*Maiye! Maiye!*" she wept aloud. "I've longed and prayed for this glad day. When Lena died we lost you. We did not hear anything! We knew nothing. We thought you all must have died. Where's Akim, my child? Why didn't he write?"

"*Tata* died soon after we got up there. We didn't have anybody—anybody. How we cried for *Tata* and *Umame!*

We were among heathen. Many went quite naked. We cried, oh, how we cried!"

Their tears were mingling now, and they were almost oblivious of the Dona's presence. But she was sympathetic and understood. After a while she left them alone. The two had a wonderful three days together.

There was so much to tell that evening at Miriam's house. They all wept at the plight of the little orphans as Alice told the mournful story. It was hard for a good, kind, unselfish woman like Miriam to justify or even be tolerant with the voracity of Nyamukalongo. Then when Alice told of the finding of that one lonely pillowcase in the midst of the wreckage of splintered wood and torn papers, Miriam clasped her hands and said, "God was behind that, Alice. Be sure of that!" Again tears were streaming down her smooth cheeks. "My poor baby," she cried. "My poor little ones! Oh, how Lena would have wept if she had known."

Then there were other things to tell, of Mrs. Davy, and of this new Dona. Of the times Nyamukalongo had taken *lobola* for her marriage to just any old Tom, Dick, or Harry who offered the most cattle.

"Don't marry, Alice, unless you marry for love," Miriam said, her eyes resting lovingly for a moment on her husband's pleasant, intelligent face.

Strange words these, to Alice, whose life had been surrounded with such coarse, obscene customs of marriage that these words from a relative were music indeed.

"Why, that's what my Dona said," the girl cried. "She said it is better never to marry than to marry as many of the Africans do! My people are all very angry. They say I'm refusing fine offers, and they will never eat my *lobola*.'"

"What does that matter?" protested Miriam angrily, 'What is a feast in comparison to happiness? Would they sell you to a life of misery just to glut themselves?"

44

"Yes, they would. I know they would," Alice answered slowly. "But I'm safe, Miriam. My Dona will not let them trouble me. They're afraid to trouble me, and I'm so glad. I'll never go back—never."

"But what of your marriage someday?" pursued Miriam. "You will marry sometime!"

"Dona said that if I let the Lord lead out in my life, He will lead me into happiness I never dreamed of. I get lots of letters from boys, but Dona says it cheapens me to write to them. Then, you know, I'm a Christian. I want my husband, if I ever have one, to be a civilized Christian too."

"Of course," assented Miriam.

Miriam's neat house was a delight to Alice, who could only dimly remember their happy home in Johannesburg, near the City Deep Hospital. Clean polished floors, a neat table with a snowy cloth, a china closet with pretty dishes. The bedrooms were neat and orderly, with smooth bedspreads, fluffy pillows, and curtained windows.

The dung-smeared huts of *Tata*'s people arose before her eyes; the fetid odor of filthy blankets; the baskets smeared with black nkhungu, so the stiff mush would not leak out; everybody reaching into one dish, pawing, rolling, and gobbling. She held her head higher. These—these—were her people. And she had almost missed this glad hour. If she had gone that day with Nedson—if Dona hadn't come and stopped her- She caught her breath at the very thought.

Two weeks later they were in Fish Hoek, a suburb of Cape Town, that curves around False Bay and half climbs up the encircling mountains. Alice worked gladly, so her Dona could rest and get well.

Sometimes they took long walks, and tried to identify some of the lovely wild flowers common to the Cape. They picked up shells on the shore. They window-shopped eagerly. The days were like bright beads strung on a golden chain of joy.

Once they drove far out to the place where the warm waters of the Indian Ocean mingle with the cold Atlantic.

"Just try to think," Dona said to Alice. "The clumsy caravels of Vasco da Gama sailed past here. Hottentots stood on these shores and watched them with wonder. Bartholomeu Dias stopped here, afraid, and turned back. Captain Cook stopped here on his third voyage. Your own ancestors, the Xosa people, lived just over that range of mountains! "

"Oh, you make history sound so interesting, Dona," cried Alice. "Tell me more!"

And so passed the days, until one day in Cape Town, Dona and Bwana met an old friend, E. L. Cardey, who was at that time director of the Voice of Prophecy in South Africa. After they had talked for a while, he leaned forward and whispered to Dona.

"Who is that pretty African girl?"

"That is Alice, whom I brought with me to help me do my work," replied Dona.

"Is she well educated?"

"Oh, yes, and she is still in school."

"There is a boy, a fine young man, at the Voice of Prophecy 1 would like her to meet. He has been praying for the Lord to open the way for him to find a good Christian wife."

"Oh, I am not looking for a match for her now," protested Dona. "There's plenty of time for that!"

"Of course you're not. But don't get your prejudices up until you see him. He is truly a fine young Christian. You'll not find many like him!"

Then he told them of how the young man had been praying for the Lord to lead him in the matter of marriage. Not just any girl would do; he prayed for an educated girl of high moral character, who could be a true helpmate to him in his lifework. One night he had had a dream. Again the problem of finding a wife came before him. "Never fear, my boy," a voice had said. "I have chosen you a wife from a faraway country." Then he awoke. Somehow, then, he was satisfied that his problem was in hands stronger than his own. He had let the matter rest.

"You come over Thursday night," said the good pastor. "We are going to a nearby town, where I want -to show a temperance moving picture to the people of the Cape Field area. Bring Alice. I would like them to see,, each other, at any rate. My boy is just as good as your girl," he teased,

"Oh, do you think so?" laughed Dona.

Then, on arriving home, Dona told Alice all about the conversation.

At first she was highly amused, and laughed heartily.

"I'm happy, Dona, just working for you and Bwana. I've been bargained for and *lobola*ed so much that I'm sick of the thought of marriage. You've saved me much sorrow and misery. I'd rather be *mbeta* [unmarried]."

"Well, let's not say that, but we do have a kind invitation to see a good moving picture, and just meeting this strange young man doesn't mean you have to marry him," Dona answered laughing.

"Just the same, I'm happy as I am—happier than I ever was in my life!"

was the girl's reply.

The pastor's home, on Thursday night, was the fore-arranged meeting place. From there they were to go to the Elsie's River Town Hall, where the film was to be shown.

Just as they arrived, the young man Pastor Cardey was sponsoring came down the street. He had a room in the servants' quarters of the pastor's house. There was the pastor on the spot, full of geniality and good humor, ready to introduce them. His eyes sparkled with fun.

"Hulme, this is Alice, Mrs. Edwards' girl, of whom I told you. Alice, this is Hulme Siwundhla, who takes care of the printing of our lessons at the Voice of Prophecy. I think Mrs. Edwards told me your mother was of the Xosa tribe. Hulme is from that tribe too."

Alice soberly shook hands with the young man. She noted clear, honest, brown eyes, the frank, intelligent face, his neat cleanliness, and quiet good taste. Alice had been trained and trained and trained in just these things. She had learned to value them.

"How do you do?" she murmured politely, as Dona had taught her to do.

On the way to the church there was an opportunity for them to talk together. Hulme himself told her what Pastor Cardey had already told her Dona.

I have been praying earnestly for God to help me meet a well-educated, refined Christian girl," he ventured shyly. "Maybe you are the one. I believe you are!"

"Oh, I'm quite sure I'm not," Alice protested perversely. "You see, my home is very, very far away. That makes it impossible for such a thing to be."

I wouldn't say so," he answered quietly. Then he told her of his dream. "The voice said from a far country. I cannot forget that!"

Soon they were at Elsie's River. The moving picture told the story of the tragic career of young Stephen C. Foster; of how strong drink and intemperance destroyed him even at the very height of his genius as a composer.

When the song I Dream of Jeanie With the Light Brown Hair," with its liquid beauty, came pouring into the room, it seemed to say to the young man, "Alice, with the dark brown hair." For Hulme was a praying young man, an earnest young man, and to him this pretty, clever brown maiden from a "far" country meant only one thing: God *had* answered his prayers. He lived so near to the Lord that he knew with a clarity difficult to understand that God had heard him and brought this wondrous thing to pass. So, before they parted that evening he said softly, "Do not fill your heart and mind full of prejudices, Alice, but pray about this. I too will pray."

What kind of young man was this? Alice couldn't help wondering all the way to Fish Hoek that evening with Dona and Bwana. She had never had much to say to

Christian young men. But the heathen were always offering "tea money," cheap bangles, beads, and sugar cane. There were always dark hints about dances here and dances there, where *mtwala* flowed freely, to be drunk for only halfpennies. Cigarettes were sold twelve for a penny. Such was the life into which Nyamukalongo would have initiated her. But this. "Pray about this, Alice. I too will pray." When she was getting ready to go to her room that night, Dona stopped her.

"Bwana and I both feel strangely about this young man, Alice. We feel that he is good, and refined and intelligent, as the pastor said. Pray about this, for we must not run before the Lord. The ways of God are 'past finding out.

"Why, *he* said that too!" Alice exclaimed in surprise. "What shall I pray for, Dona?"

"Only for guidance, my dear. Only that God Will lead you. I too will pray. This is just as astonishing to me as it is to you. Let us not make any effort to further this thing at all. Let us just let God lead out."

"All right, Dona," replied the girl. "Good night."

"Good night, Alice."

Then for a month they were away from Cape Town at a big junior camp near French Hoek. Dona and Bwana were counselors, and Alice helped in the kitchen and with the dishes and made herself generally beloved and useful.

She washed clothes in the river, happily beating the sweaty dust out on smooth stones. Often little girls and boys gathered around her and she told them thrilling stories of her faraway country, where lions and leopards roamed the bush and snakes got into the houses. She taught them to twist their small tongues into the songs of Zion in Cinyanja, until even the smallest could go around the camp singing, "Jesus is coming again."

> "Abweranso!
> Abweranso!
> Yesu adzabweranso!"

She tried to help everyone. She darted here and there, washing shirts and dresses, ironing, pressing, sweeping, cleaning, always smiling and happy. Everyone liked her.

After a while they were home again—this time to a house in Claremont, near to the division offices. It was a restful place. The rooms were cool and quiet, and there was a grassy garden behind the house. Alice had the whole place immaculate by eight o'clock. Then she settled down with algebra, geometry, and English composition. For Alice's schoolwork must go on even though she was far away from Malamulo.

Watermelon and grape season was in full swing. What varied delicacies the tired missionaries enjoyed! On the Sabbath days they went to the Cape Mission Field churches, which were under Pastor A. C. LeButt's kindly care. Alice made many friends with these earnest people.

The Cape colored people are great lovers of flowers. The whole street by the Cape Town post office is a flower bazaar. Their lawns and the gardens of their houses are riots of gorgeous color. They seem to have an almost fanatical love of beauty.

Every one of their churches is a bower of beauty, made so by the many flowers brought in to decorate the house of God. The effect is pleasing to behold.

Hulme wrote to Alice occasionally, always pressing his belief that God must have had a hand in their meeting. Alice answered the letters politely, but made no further effort to allow him to see her. This had been her and Dona's agreement. God must lead, and in such a signal way that there could be no doubt that He *was* leading.

One Sunday, Alice had studied algebra, geometry, and arithmetic all day. Her spirits were drooping with weariness. It was about four in the afternoon. Dona stepped to the kitchen door.

"Enough of study, now, my child," she said. "I want company for a walk. Bwana is sleeping; Daddy Lee has gone for a walk. You need the air. Wash your face and come on.

So the two of them sallied forth for a quiet evening stroll. Up toward the Claremont business section they usually bent their footsteps, so they could window-shop. No stores, except confectioneries, were open, because it was Sunday. Slowly they walked, enjoying each window display. It was a treat for eyes long accustomed to the stores of dry Nyasaland.

"There, see that sweater, Dona!" exclaimed Alice, "I'll knit one like that for you when we get home."

"Oh, that will be very nice! But look at those shoes, Alice. Two ankle straps. Must be a new style."

"Oh, yes, it is," cried Alice. "The girls in Wynberg were wearing them. They're so pretty."

49

So they went up one side of the *main* street and down the other side, until they were almost ready to turn and go home, when——

"Why—good afternoon!"

It was Hulme standing, looking at them politely, his hat in his hand—his heart in his eyes.

"Why, good afternoon, Hulme. How are you?" Dona was cordial with him, but Alice stood back shyly.

"I'm fine, madam, but so sorry I have not been able to see any of you for so long." His eyes were on Alice's face.

"How are you, Miss Alice?" he asked shyly. "I'm sorry I haven't seen you for so long."

Then Hulme asked Dona if she could come and give a talk in his church. After they had talked for a while, she agreed, but she told him that she did not know the way, and Bwana could not go with her, since he had a meeting already scheduled for that day.

"I know what," he said, his eyes shining, "if I knew where you lived, I'd come early Sabbath morning and show you the way to the Langa church." Dona told him he'd better come along, so he could find out where they lived.

They walked home then, Alice chattering about this and that to hide her self-consciousness. When he was certain he knew the way, Hulme went his way politely. He was never presumptuous in any way.

Alice stood very still in the middle of the kitchen after he had gone.

"He is nice," she said thoughtfully. "He's so polite, and so gentle. Did you see him take my arm when we got to that muddy place in the road? I was so surprised. I have never seen an African man do that. I've seen Europeans do it, but never one of my own people."

The next day circumstances arose that made it impossible for Dona to go to Langa on that particular Sabbath.

That afternoon she called Hulme by telephone, so that he could make other arrangements.

"Oh, that is unfortunate," said the voice at the other end of the wire.

"But, I can, as you say, make the arrangements. "But, madam——"

"Yes, Hulme?

"May I take Alice to church at Rondebosch, near your home? I'll get her back home as quickly as you get back from your appointment."

"That's all right, Hulme. I'll tell her."

"Thank you, madam. Good-by."

"Good-by."

After Hulme brought Alice home from the church at Rondebosch, he had another request ready.

"Madam, may I come tomorrow and take Alice to see the zoo? I will come about one, and I'll get her home by fivethirty."

"You must ask Alice whether she would like to go," Dona told him with a smile.

"Oh, I already have," he replied, looking mischievously at Alice.

"I'd like to go, Dona," Alice offered quietly.

The trip to the zoo was made, and other harmless little excursions. Sometimes it was prayer meeting at one of the Cape Field churches; at other times, an entertainment given by one of the churches. All of these offered opportunities for pleasant, clean association and closer acquaintance.

But the time drew near when Dona and Bwana had to leave the Cape and go back to Malamulo. The beautiful Cape furlough was almost over. Alice was quiet those days as she went about her work or studied her lessons. A new experience had come into her young life. She came to know what it was to begin to care for someone. She confided in her Dona as they worked together in the kitchen or as they sat sewing or mending after the ironing.

"It is so strange, Dona," she would say. "I don't understand my own feelings. I did not know people ever felt the way I do. People just picked husbands for girls in our villages, and they had to marry them. There was no choice. I know some of them quite hate the cruel, ignorant men who are chosen. But they can't help themselves."

"In God's plan, Alice," Dona answered, "a husband and a wife should love each other so much that the home they establish is like a little heaven on earth."

"I am learning that, Dona," the girl answered quietly. "And that is the kind of home I want. I remember our mother used to kiss us in Johannesburg. But once I heard some heathen laughing at the custom of kissing. They said, 'Who wants a mouth smeared with food or spittle slobbering on his face?' I remember reading that the custom has existed since Bible times. My poor people have lost the love out of marriage!"

One evening, after Hulme had brought her home from prayer meeting, Alice sought Dona breathlessly. Dona was in the dining room, putting in water some flowers someone in Wynberg had given her at prayer meeting. Tenderly she was arranging colorful dahlias in a wide vase.

"Dona, Dona!" the girl whispered.

"Yes, Alice."

"O Dona! I don't know what to say! Tonight after the prayer meeting he asked me to marry him."

"What does your heart tell you to say, Alice."

"My heart says 'Yes' but my head says 'No.' I don't want to live here. There are no schools here where I can teach *my* people. I've dedicated my life to teaching African children. O Dona, what can I do? What can I do? Was there ever a girl who had to decide such hard things? "

"Oh, yes, Alice. In everyone's life there come times of hard decisions. But we have a Father in heaven who can arrange everything. He knows the end from the beginning."

"Yes, Dona, that is true, for Hulme told me to pray about it. We had prayer together this evening. He said we are both faced with many difficulties, for there are customs of all kinds we must meet and overcome. But God is strong, and He can help us if it is His will that this thing can be."

"I too will pray, Alice."

It has been two long years since those two young lovers bade each other a tearful farewell. They were pledged to each other, with prayers that God would open the way for them to be married and labor together in the work of God.

The ways of God are wonderful. Hulme has had a call now to leave his home country and labor in this union. He will be a missionary, and Alice too will be in the blessed work of God.

One of these days, there will be a wedding in the Malamulo church. And Alice, who has had *lobola* paid for her many times, will marry for love. And I think that in that new home which is soon to be established, she will put a clean starched pillowcase on a pillow, with loving thoughts of *Umame*. For she says she wants a home where love dwells, such as *Umame* had, and such as her new white mother has. It has been a long, long road, a hard road, since she was left alone among the heathen. But God had never lost sight of His precious little Alice. He brought her through the darkness, that she might know and love the light—the beautiful light.

DE BEER
SETTLED FOR
BLACK DIAMONDS

African Terms Not Translated in the Text

Grootmoeder–grandmother

Huisvrou–housewife

Ja, Gerrie, maar eksal nou maar bly tot jy klaarys–Yes, go and finish your explanation

Rooibostee–red bush tea

Tante, die tyd is nou op–Auntie, the time is now up

Tante, kom binne vir tien minuute–Auntie, come in for ten minutes

Vrou–wife

Tribal Terms

Indaba–a trial

Nkos–sir

Nkosikazi–madam

De Beer Settled
for Black Diamonds

They told us to meet Elder de Beer in Queenstown, John de Beer, who was president of the South Bantu Mission Field. So we drove over the hot, dusty road till Queenstown lay before us, scorched and dusty too, sweltering and panting under the ravages of a long and terrible drought. The Royal Hotel-short, squat but clean, suffered too from the drought. Baths were rationed. No tub baths were allowed. We who think of baths almost as we think of drinking, or eating, could only take "spit baths" after the hot winds had seared us and the boiling sun had baked us and the flying dust had ground into us all day.

We had no sooner settled in the big double room opening onto a long cool veranda than we heard the gong of the dinner bell. It was there that we met Elder de Beer and his wife. Very often a person feels reserved and wary upon meeting a person for the first time, but not so in this instance. From the very first moment of meeting, we felt that the De Beers fitted snugly in a niche in our hearts, and that they had always been there, God bless them.

Of course, I was curious about them, for I had heard something about this remarkable family and of the outstanding events connected with their experience in the promulgation of the third angel's message. This is the story told me by this grand old man.

Kimberley, the center of the Griqualand West diamond industry, was founded in 1870, shortly after diamonds were found in that region. In 1867, when all South Africa was sunk in financial depression, a farmer, Schalk van Niekerk, visited a friend's home near the Orange River. As he sat talking to his friends the Jacobses, he observed that their children were playing a game called five stones, and one of their playthings was very bright and glittering.

When Van Niekerk expressed surprise and admiration for the stone, the children's mother gave it to him. Van Niekerk was overjoyed with his gift.

"Oh, you can have it, if you like it," she had said.

Soon after that Van Niekerk took the stone to a trader, who told him to take it to a Dr. Atherstone, a mineralogist in Cape Town.

It was declared to be a diamond, and it was sold for five hundred pounds. Van Niekerk gave half of it to his friends, the Jacobses.

Schalk van Niekerk was convinced that there was an alluvial diamond bed in that vicinity, and kept his ears and eyes open. By quizzing here and questioning there, he learned another piece of news in 1869.

He heard of a native witch doctor who had a large shining charm to which he attributed all kinds of supernatural powers. Van Niekerk's suspicions were aroused. He immediately investigated the matter, suspecting that the stone might be a diamond. It was as he thought. It was indeed a diamond so large that, uncut, it weighed eighty-three carats. It was later sold to the Earl of Dudley for twenty-five thousand pounds, and was so brilliant and lovely that it was called the "Star of South Africa." The poor, dirty old witch doctor who found it got cattle worth about two hundred pounds for one of the most beautiful diamonds in all the world.

And there in the neighborhood, right where that great strike was made, lived Johannes Nicolas de Beer and his family. It was the year 1870. Of course they had heard of the diamond strike on the nearby Dutoitspan and Bultfontein farms. But old Johannes had work to do there at Vooruitzight farm, and didn't have time for gewgaws and luxuries the rich might delight in. Cattle herded by little black boys and sheep browsing over his veld must be looked after. Maize must be sown and reaped down in the oozy black land bordering the river. But while old Johannes worked from dawn to dark, strange men prowled stealthily about his acres and fields—money-hungry men, who were searching for great rough circular depressions of ground covered with yellowish or bluish sod. These eagle-eyed experts knew that under this yellow and blue topsoil was a big funnel or crater, rich in that most precious of all stones. And in their stealthy prowling they found it there at Vooruitzight, a richer find by far than in any of the other places. Diamonds worth many millions of dollars lay under the harsh, rocky fields and rolling veld. How would Johannes know that one of the richest mines in all the world lay under his calloused feet?

Old Johannes was a godly man, and an elder in the Dutch Reformed Church. His children were strictly reared and were taught to work as soon as they were old enough to lift a hoe. Often Johannes or Gert Pettus or one of his other sons or daughters would find a brilliant, lovely stone dug out of a molehill or in the earth raked out when the dam was built. They would pocket them and set them on the mantel for a day or two. It was pleasant to see the gleaming brightness of a rough stone there. Even if the house was darkened, it shone and glittered like an evil eye in a witch's woods. But old *Vrou* de Beer was a scrupulous housekeeper, and tossed the "rocks" out in disgust when she scoured and cleaned the place, grumbling and sputtering about the "fetching in of dirty junk and trash to muddy up her clean house."

And it was to this spotless Dutch farmstead some buyers came one day. After much hemming and hawing they offered old Johannes a measly three thousand pounds for his farm, and desired immediate possession.

They flattered the good old man, stressing in loud tones the fine work he'd done there—that they were impressed by the *place* and wanted to settle down. Wily old foxes! If the De Beers had held out for hundreds of times that price, the buyers would have purchased it, for only four years later the same farm was bought by the state for one hundred thousand pounds.

De Beer and his wife were sitting out in the shade by the house when the men came up to give Johannes their offer for his farm. The house was large and comfortable, built with high gables and the tight Dutch thatch roofcool in summer and warm in winter. In building, these home-loving Dutch were eager to transplant a bit of their beloved Netherlands to the hot, dry bush and and wastelands of South Africa!

Johannes was sitting in his armchair, enjoying the shade of the wattle trees he had planted and cosseted with his own gnarled hands. *Huisvrou* de Beer was knitting strong socks, her old hands almost as hard as pine boards from scrubbing her benches and tables with lye leached from her own wood ashes. The soft wool stuck to her harsh fingers, yet they were skillful and true in turning heels and fashioning toes with even, perfect stitches.

The old mother looked at the strangers suspiciously. She had a streak of astuteness that old Johannes did not possess. So, when the three thousand pounds was offered, she drew up her mouth tightly and knitted all the faster.

Three thousand pounds! More money than they'd ever possessed in their whole hard-working lives! Enough to buy a much bigger, much better farm! Johannes' eyes glittered. He opened his mouth to answer quickly in the affirmative. Then to his amazement and chagrin, his wife spoke up defiantly. That woman! she'd spoil a good sale yet!

" You offer us three thousand pounds? Yes? Well, no! That is too little for this farm we've worked and toiled and improved now these many years, Johannes and I. It is six thousand five hundred, or you can't touch it. No!"

Johannes gasped. Was the woman crazy? Whoever heard of such an outlandish price? He felt the anger well up in him at her silly meddling. What did she know about men's business? He took his long Dutch pipe from his mouth, preparatory to silencing her sharply, when Epton, the prospective buyer, answered her quickly—almost too quickly, if they'd thought.

"Six thousand five hundred pounds, you say? Very well. We will pay. We are very interested in your farm. That price is not too far off."

The deal was closed, with old Johannes and his wife getting only the barest fraction of what the place was actually worth. How were they to know that this farm, *Vooruitzight*, was to contain an amazing pile of diamonds, the most valuable in all the world? How was Johannes to know that right near to where he sat under his trees to sign the papers, there would be a great yawning hole, and that shafts would be sunk more than twenty-six hundred feet deep before a score of years should pass!

Johannes gave possession as soon as he could. The great canvas-covered *voortrekker* wagons were inspanned with many oxen, and all their possessions were stored away inside. There were the charcoal irons with little doors into which one put fire; the tongs, the candle molds and the big iron pots in which they boiled their meats and stews. *Huisvrou* brought along roots and seeds and starters of all kinds.

With his money Johannes bought a great stretch of land bordering along the Vaal River. It was so large that when old Johannes finally died on his new Orange Free State farm, and it was divided, every son and daughter of his was given a large farm. He lived a godly life, and did everything, in his power, as he thought God wanted him to do. His children loved him and believed in him. Even now, though he has been dead for many years, the fragrance of his godly life still lingers. He lived up to all the light he had.

The day he died all of his children were standing around, sad and disconsolate, waiting for the dreaded time when they must tell their father good-by for the last time.

It was the mother who called them.

"Come," she had said, her face drawn, wrinkled, and old under the neat white Dutch cap, "father is calling you. Come quickly."

Then they crowded into the small bedroom, as quietly as their rough shoes would allow them. Old Johannes was sunk down in the homemade bed, so gaunt and thin that his body hardly raised the bedclothes. His great beard, flecked with white, lay on his chest. He opened his eyes and gazed at them for a moment or two.

"'Fear God, and keep his commandments,'" he said in a weak, faraway voice; "'for this is the whole duty of man.'"

It might have been a Moses giving a last word to his people, or a Joshua

58

giving sturdy counsel to those who must go on warring. For even as they watched the old man with tear-streaked faces, Johannes closed his blue eyes and went to his last, long sleep. And his children knew, looking at his face, calm and dignified in death, that if there is a God—a hereafter, and a reward for the righteous—old Johannes would have a part.

Then the home place was divided, and the eldest son, Gert Pettus, and his young wife, were given the share on which the widowed mother lived. A neat little brick house was built near the old home, and there they started what they thought would be a serene married life.

About this time some strange things began to happen among the relatives that upset the whole family.

There was their cousin, Peter Wessels, as conscientious a man as one would ever meet, who had become involved in the most insane Bible notions one had ever heard of. And Peter had been so well thought of too. He had such strong belief in prayer that several people had been healed when he prayed for them. People had confidence in him, although many of them thought he was a little too strict, and told him so. For instance, Peter had been a strict Sundaykeeper. One day his brother John was laughing at him for turning his windmill off so it wouldn't "work" on the "Sabbath."

"The Sabbath!" John had laughed. "That's really fanatical, Peter. Sunday's not the Sabbath of the Lord! Don't be so ignorant!"

"If Sunday is not the Sabbath, then tell me what day is!" Peter countered sharply.

"Why, Peter, *Saturday* is the only Sabbath the Bible teaches. If you don't believe it, read your Bible! I've often been surprised at you. Making your windmill and wagons and oxen rest on Sunday! Hah! You're as bad as the Jews were!"

"But John!" Peter had hotly protested, "if I do anything or keep anything, I want to do it or keep it right. I want to follow what God says to the very letter! I want to—"

"Well, see that you know what God says, then," his brother observed laconically.

As a result this honest man began an intensive study of God's Holy Word. With concordance and Bible, Peter spent many hours perusing the doctrines of the Bible, until, to the discomfiture of his family in general, he began to keep the Sabbath. It wasn't long until, as a result of his intensive persuasiveness, his whole family accepted the Sabbath truth and the Advent message, and in the heart of Africa their beacon shone out bright as a light shining in a dark place.

About thirty miles from the De Beer farm lived an ardent Sabbathkeeper named Scholtz. Many of his neighbors had tried to "set him right," only to have him turn a deaf ear to their comments. Naturally, they didn't hanker after another encounter. All good orthodox Dutch Reformed members were urged to stay clear, for he would not keep quiet. He would foist his strange doctrine upon everyone until people were afraid of him.

Gert Pettus, the eldest son, one day volunteered to go with his sister-in-law to see Scholtz concerning a business transaction. She was afraid to go alone, for he "opened up his Biblical Gatling guns" on every soul who came around for any reason. It wasn't safe.

"Why, yes, sister, I'll go with you," Gert had said. "You go tell the boys to inspan, and I'll be ready in about half an hour. I know quite a bit about the Bible myself, and I'll just take the wind out of that smart aleck's sails in less time than it takes to tell it."

Gert went up to his room and spread his father's cumbersome Dutch Bible out on the table. Then with a pencil, and a great deal of sweating, searching, and leafing to and fro, he managed to get a few texts jotted down on an old envelope. "That'll settle him," he chuckled. "He won't expect to have five or six good texts like these slung right down his gullet in the middle of his argument. He'll not get me down."

So, with every evidence of "thinking he was standing," Gert Pettus de Beer clambered over the great iron-bound wheel beside his sister-in-law and settled down to a journey that was to be his Marathon, his Waterloo, and his Damascus road. The road was hot and long, and several times the two took big swigs from the demijohn that grandmother had filled with calabash milk before they left. It was a cooling drink made of milk, clabbered down in a big calabash gourd. There's nothing that tastes quite like it. Once you sample a little you're an addict.

At long last they drew near to the Scholtz farm, but it was only to see that good man clambering over the wheel of his ox wagon, preparatory to going some place himself. He stopped his oxen, alighted, and walked to meet the oncoming span.

Emitting a loud halloo, half a dozen little Kaffir boys seemed to swarm up from nowhere.

"Outspan these oxen," he ordered.

"*Ewe, Baas,*" they sang out, little black hands already at work.

"You, Martje," he told the sister-in-law, "you go to the house and see the womenfolks. Gert and I, we are going over to the next farm on a bit of an errand. We'll see you after a while."

"If you want a cool drink, Gert," he said, "get one off the porch. There's a pot cooling there, but hurry, we want to get back before chores."

Gert felt for his envelope, after he'd quenched his thirst. It was there. All his ammunition was intact. He felt very sure of himself as he hurried back to the wagon and to Scholtz. And away they went over the rough veld, to the farm buildings that seemed to be like a handful of toys swimming in the heat of the broiling sun. Drawing near, they could hear the shouts of the herdsboys, driving the cattle to the dam for water. Then Scholtz stopped the oxen by a few harsh bushes growing out of the stony ground.

"I am going to pray for a while," he told Gert. "You come pray with me. I need wisdom when I present the Word of God to my unbelieving neighbors." Gert's heart almost stopped beating. He'd walked right into a trap with both eyes open. Yet, calling himself a Christian, strict and orthodox, how could he refuse to pray if a man asked him.

They knelt behind a rocky copse and the good man asked Gert to pray first. The situation was so strange that Gert hardly knew what to pray about. He prayed about this and that so vaguely that it seemed to one listening that he was just filling the air with well-worn phrases without praying for anything at all.

Not so with Scholtz, however. Gert opened his eyes and looked at him curiously as they knelt there. He held his head up, and addressed God as one speaks to a personal friend. He talked on smoothly, softly, confidently, never lacking a word, or stumbling, asking for wisdom and guidance when he presented truths "not to be denied." Gert thought of the envelope in his pocket, which he'd prepared for the denials of this truth "not to be denied."

He followed Scholtz into the house, feeling like a horse thief. If this were error, it would seem to these good people as if he were an accomplice in a web of deceit—conniving without conscience in the propagation of error. He felt like a dog. He *was* a dog! But there was one good thing: he could hear what Scholtz had to say, and he'd be doing God a service to set this poor benighted creature right.

"Well, I'm come, Brother and Sister Potgieter," Scholtz began when they were seated, "to let you know just why I'm keeping Saturday as I do. Now, you get your Bibles, and if you can find any texts to set me right, I'll listen, but I'm going to set you right according to my understanding of God's Word."

Gert smiled and stealthily drew his envelope from his inside pocket. He'd take Scholtz up right here and now, for he'd talked a little too fast that time.

61

And then he began so rapidly that Gert was as confused as if he'd been hit over the head with an ox goad. He looked down at his envelope in dismay. Mr. Scholtz was using the *very* texts to prove Sabbathkeeping that he had brought to prove Sundaykeeping. Gert felt every prop knocked out from under him. Then Scholtz's voice grew soft and persuasive. Gert looked at his friends, the Potgieters, sitting there under the piercing barrage of truth. Pieter sat, his great shaggy head down and his dark beard caressing his broad chest. He was searching perplexedly through his Bible. Then his great horny hands became curiously relaxed, as if it was no use to fight. Elspeth, his wife, sat, her face sober and pinched, her deep-sunk eyes squinted with thinking.

"And now," Scholtz resumed, laying his Bible down and looking earnestly at his friends, "I've tried to show you what I believe God's requirements for man are. I've written all over trying to get the great men to give me good reasons from God's Word for keeping Sunday, but not one could do it. Not one. All I got was abuse for leaving the church of my fathers. If you, Brother Potgieter, or you, Brother de Beer, have any such proofs up your sleeves, it is your duty before God to show me my error."

Gert looked at his thumbed, creased envelope and searched his mind for something to say to vindicate himself. But nothing came to his lips. The fountain was dry. Nor did a word come from the other couple for a while. Then Potgieter lifted his head.

"I've not had much book learning myself, but 1 know you must be speaking the truth, for I too have tried to find ways of getting out of this. We all know we're headed for trouble in the family and among the neighbors if we accept, and trouble with God if we don't. So I don't see but that we'd better do what God says. I hadn't wanted to believe this, Scholtz, and I was sorry for a while you'd told us. But then Elspeth said last night that we can't hide our heads in the sand like the ostriches; we must face it, and thank God for this new light'"

Tears were streaming down Scholtz's face when he finished.

"God be praised, God be praised! Let us pray!" But Gert had escaped from the room; so he missed the prayer and praise meeting that followed in that little room. He walked to and fro near the big kraal where Potgieter kept his cattle at night. Off across the seas of rippling dry grass he could see the giant boulders lying in the stream bed below the dam, and the blinding shine of water, spilling over the dam. He saw it, but he didn't see it. What he saw was his own heart, hard as the stones beneath the dam. It seemed as if it would be as hard to soften his hard heart as for the water flowing endlessly over the dam to soften those boulders. And yet, he knew, yes he knew right now that the words he had heard were true. That Bible study given by Scholtz cleared his mind as a harsh electrical storm clears the thick, dry air of the veld before a great rain shower washes his little world. And it was as frightening too. Every text, given so surely, was a great, blinding, jagged slash through the serene blue of his firmament, and left him unnerved and trembling. What was he to do? What was he to say? How was he to react to this new way of thinking?

How he got home he never quite knew. Martje was meddlesome and annoying, trying to pry the details of his victory over Scholtz from him. But he had been noncommittal enough and answered her in monosyllables. Wouldn't the woman's tongue stop clacking? He wanted to think.

He threw the reins, without thought, to the half dozen pickaninnies who had run up to outspan. Then he strode to the house without a word. The kitchen was immaculately clean. An African girl was scrubbing black pots with ashes and gravel out by the water drums. Another was washing some dish towels by soaping them and pounding and pummeling them vigorously on a smooth stone. Inside the house the table was laid for supper. His wife was stirring clotted cream into a great dish of Dutch cheese, from which the whey had only then been pressed. He could hear the mutton roast sputtering in its juices in the big covered pot that had been pulled from the coals of the fireplace. He knew potatoes had been cooked with the meat, and browned in the juices. A crusty loaf and a sharp knife lay on the wooden breadboard on the corner of the table. A candle was burning on a high cupboard, the flame pointing off sideways a little, because the breath of evening air came in through the open door. The room was full of shadows, gaunt and distorted. Gert's little boys were washing, making their splattery, bubbly ablutions on the long bench by the door, using a piece of hard brown soap, made by his wife's clever hands. From the looks of the long, coarse towel, but little of the dirt was left in the water, for most of it seemed to have been wiped off on the length of linen crash hung there for family scrub-ups. The old *grootmoeder* came in just then, her face placid and satisfied in the candlelight. Her cap was snowy white, and she had tied on a fresh apron edged with crocheted lace.

Into this peaceful scene Gert came with his poor heart in a veritable turmoil.

He filled the plates with sliced meat, roasted potatoes, gravy, and Dutch cheese. Cape gooseberry tart was there cooling, its pinkish amber juices almost escaping. It was a supper such as he loved, but tonight he was in no mood to eat, and partook sparingly of the appetizing food. Such texts as, "Remember the sabbath day, to keep it holy," and, "Hallow my sabbaths; and they shall be a sign between me and you, that ye may know that I am the Lord your God," ran repeatedly through his brain. If he had been eating ashes and mud cakes, he would hardly have known the difference.

"Gert, you're not eating'" His wife peered at him anxiously in the dim light. "Here, take a little of the tart, it is very sweet and good."

Grandmother made a tut-tutting sound with her tongue. "The sun—he is hot, and that trip by Scholtz was tiring.

The little black girl came in and passed the tarts and filled the big cups with *rooibostee*, gathered in and dried from bushes on the veld. Gert drank cupful after cupful.

For several weeks Gert's boys noticed that their father sat with his Bible every moment he could spare from his stock, fields, and dairy; just sat there, leafing here and leafing there and writing down notes on paper. Grandmother thought he might be going to die, he was getting so pious, just like a pastor. She reminded his worried wife that there had been pastors in *her* family 'way back in the old country. Most likely Gert took after her side of the house. There came a time when she would have denied that vigorously.

But *Huisvrou* de Beer shook her head sadly. "He is going mad, Mother. I know. He's not the same. He speaks gently all the time and never shouts down the help or the pickaninnies. He doesn't eat enough to keep a bird alive, and he's always reading the Bible, or perhaps leafing back and forth. It isn't natural, I know it isn't. I've heard of people going crazy over religion, haven't you?"

The conversation took place in the big farm kitchen early Saturday morning, where *Vrou* de Beer was doing her cooking for Sunday. The boys had gone out to the veld to look after ewes. It was lambing time, and John, the eldest, was a sober, responsible lad who took his duties seriously- Old Grandmother sat in a chair, her lean, hard hands busy with her endless knitting.

Gert was in the sitting room with his Bible as usual. Suddenly, he called his wife and mother to him. They exchanged anxious glances before they went slowly into his presence.

Then Gert called some native yard boys who were sweeping the dooryard with twig brooms.

"You pickaninnies! go just now, and get the boys!"

"*Ewe, Baas!*" they cried, and off scampered half a dozen pairs of little hard black feet to get the boys of the Baas to come home for some unknown, mysterious reason.

John is now a gray-haired man, but he still remembers the fear that gripped his heart that Saturday morning when he and his brothers scampered across the harsh grass and rocks for home. Mother's and grandmother's voices were both lifted in high, discordant wailing. Who was dead, or dying? father? sister? Auntie Martje? Halfdazed with fear, with feet like wooden clumps that refused to obey their wills, the boys stumbled into the familiar sitting room. Something was burning on the hearth, but no one heeded. The air was full of a pungent smell like burning feathers. Granny and mother were weeping in the bedroom. The boys stood there, fumbling frayed Kaffir hats in their dirty hands.

Father looked up.

"Sit down, boys," he said, simply. Their eyes never left their father's grim face.

Mother came to the bedroom door.

"O my dear children!" she exclaimed. Then turning to her husband she cried out accusingly, "Gert, you've gone wrong yourself, and now you're not satisfied till you lead my children with you into the path of destruction!" Then she cried, "O God help us! God help us!"

But Gert ignored the wailing sounds in the bedroom and turned toward the boys, who sat trembling on the rough homemade chairs.

"Boys," he said, "boys, we've never kept the Sabbath. Today—Saturday— is the Sabbath of the Lord. We're going to keep it, God helping us!"

Then he opened his Bible and began reading to them from many places in which he had stuck paper bookmarks. John often has said, in telling this, that there never had been a family worship like this one. Every word his father read or uttered went through him like an electric shock. Gert Petrus ignored completely the heaving sobs in the bedroom.

"My boys," he said, "I've been studying this matter a long time. Yet I wanted to make sure; so I wrote to Pastor Rossourv, head of the church in this part of Africa. I wanted to get every side of it."

"Oh, did you, Father?" John asked eagerly. "And what did he say?"

"The answer came only today, my son," Gert answered patiently. "That is why I called you. Listen, I'll read you what he said," and Gert picked up a big envelope from the table in front of him, opened the letter, and hurriedly scanned the contents.

"I won't read it all," he said, his eyes on the paper.

"Only what's important. Oh, yes, here it is: 'Brother de Beer, you are getting exercised and unduly wrought up over trivialities. Of course, we have no Scriptural basis for the Sunday as we keep it; it is a tradition of the church, too strongly rooted to be changed. And really, what is the difference? We give God one day, a day established on the memory and beauty of His resurrection from the dead—so why worry? Our fathers held to this faith, and are we better than those who led us?'"

Gert folded the letter and returned it to the envelope. "It is not a good excuse," he said reasonably, "for us to follow traditions rather than the commandments of God. I'm surprised at our pastors, or *predikants*, for being satisfied with such. I'm not, and I'm through with the traditions of men!"

The weeping and wailing began afresh in the bedroom, and presently the old *grootmoeder* emerged, her shrunken face more dominated by anger now than grief. She shook a thin old finger in her son's face.

"All right, then, you domkop," she shrilled. "If your old father was alive still he would beat you with a sjambok till your skin would fall off!"

"No, Mother," Gert answered quietly. "Father would not lay violent hands on me, no. He was of an inquiring mind himself, and I believe he would have joined right in with me if he had seen the truth as I see it."

The old grandmother stood and looked at her son, so calm and unperturbed, while she was trembling with rage. "After all," she asked herself, "might not Gert be right? Johannes hadn't always poured into the mold just as she had liked, even though the whole neighborhood well knew that she was the one who laid down the law in that family. Every once in a while old Johannes staged a silent, unyielding rebellion that all her ranting and snorting could not touch. Just like that old *kopje* standing there on the veld, hard and unmoved, though blown by searing winds, scorched by sun, and drenched by the swift showers of pouring rain.

"Then you can *go*!" she said in anger. "Get off my land and my farm. You can't manage it for me! " But even as she spoke the words she regretted such a rash thrust, for she could travel cast to Madagascar, south to the warm waters of the Indian Ocean, west to the gray Atlantic, and never would she find anyone so faithful, and tractable, and "workbrickle" under petticoat government as Gert Petrus.

The young man lifted his honest eyes. "Yes, Mother," he said evenly, "I will go if you want to chase me away just because I want to obey the commandments of God. But I can't give it up. It is like a fire burning in my bones. I'd never see another happy moment if I gave up what I know is right."

The old mother stood there wavering, fighting a battle with her dogmatism and dominating disposition. "Well, then," she softened a little, not meeting her son's sober eyes, "well, you stay, Gert Petrus, but don't you go proselyting all over this place. Just keep still about your believing this and that."

"That, Mother, I can't do either." Gert's voice was firm, with not one

66

element of temporizing in it. The old woman knew she couldn't silence her son's tongue. Never loquacious, he wanted to be heard when he did talk. So without a word she left and went over to her own house, where she and Johannes had lived.

Gert had the boys wash up, and they got into the oxcart and went to Scholtz's for the day. Thus the air was cleared, for the time, at least.

The daughter-in-law and mother-in-law united in their opposition to Petrus and the boys. They did everything overt that they could do to discomfit and irritate him. Slighting remarks, unusual activities on Sabbath while he was trying to worship, seemed not to disturb him at all. He just kept up his silent revelation of truth before the two. At night the boys could hear their parents talking in bed. They recognized their mother's high, petulant, complaining, voice; then their father's calm reply. Every night it was the same: Gert Petrus' stolid persistence and clean-cut logic; his wife's rebellious complainings.

But it had its effect. In Mrs. de Beer's heart the conviction began to grow that Gert must be right. "Why, he must be! He's going through all kinds of persecution, and I'm instigating it! "

Suddenly she sat up and looked at her husband. "Gert! she cried. "Gert! Gert, dear! "

"Are you calling me, Mommie?" he asked, stirring uneasily.

"Yes, Gert. Wake up, do. Gert, you're right—and I won't fight you any more."

He was wide awake by now. Awkwardly he kissed his wife's wet cheeks.

"You believe, Mommie? You see?" he whispered, pressing his hard cheek against hers until their tears mingled.

"Yes, yes, Gert. Oh, yes! I'll tell mother in the morning!"

"I'll get Scholtz to hold meetings in the schoolhouse, and we'll go. I built that schoolhouse myself with bricks I burned right here. Mother would object if he gave us studies at home!" Gert told his wife.

"Yes, yes, Gert. But the schoolhouse is better; then other people can come. This is worth telling!"

They went to sleep very, very happy. The fair moon peeped into the window, glowing with pleasure at the sight of such rare happiness. She had seldom seen the like in all of her wanderings.

So poor old Grandmother de Beer was left quite alone in her fanatical zeal to "put a stop to the nonsense." Gert's wife had deserted. She felt old, tired, and sad: but indomitable! stubborn! dogmatic! Yes, those characteristics were the warp and woof of her being! Only a miracle, only re-creation, would

67

change her. But God was and is able to change even the most unpromising lumps of clay into jewels fit to adorn His lovely crown. And He was working on Grandma de Beer.

One day Grandma had to pass the schoolhouse, where Scholtz happened to be preaching. She had steered clear of the place, for she had not wanted to hear a single word of heresy. It was a sore trial, though, in a locality where there were few things to see and fewer places to go. To sit on her stoop in lonely solitude and see the people come and crowd into the schoolhouse three times a week was almost more than she could bear. She was a gregarious soul and loved to mingle and chat and gossip as well as anyone. This day the pickaninnies who were tending the geese had quite forgotten them, and she heard their honk-honking clear up to the stoop, and was moved to investigate. Her search led her past the door where neighbor Scholtz was preaching. Great charts, with pictures of mysterious, ferocious beasts, hung clear across the front of the room. Involuntarily she stopped and gazed, for she had been curious over all the mysterious goings on in the schoolhouse.

Pastor Scholtz had just begun his sermon and was reading his text in a strong, emphatic voice:

"Write the vision, and make it plain upon tables, that he may run that readeth it. For the vision is yet for an appointed time, but at the end it shall speak, and not lie: though it tarry, wait for it; because it will surely come, it will not tarry."

Just as Scholtz had finished reading his text, he espied from the corner of his eye the white-capped old Dutch woman standing-her face lifted, the interest plainly showing on her stubborn old face.

Suddenly Scholtz stepped over, and with rare tact, called kindly: "*Tante, kom binne vir tien minuute.*"

He thought that if he could coax her in for ten minutes, then he would rely on the Holy Spirit to get her so interested that she would stay.

Surprisingly, the old woman agreed. She mounted the steps with alacrity, untied her sunbonnet, and sat down. She fastened her eyes suspiciously on Scholtz, who began, with lightning speed to explain the four beasts of Daniel 7. He was not only elucidating the lion that represented Babylon but sum*mon*ing all his eloquence to beard a certain old lioness right in her den. She listened with rapt attention. Suddenly Gerrie Scholtz turned to her to remind her that the time he'd asked her to stay was up.

"*Tante, die tyd is nou op,*" he said slyly.

The old lady darted him an exasperated glance but said just as craftily, "*Ja, Gerrie, maar ek sal nou maar bly tot jy klaarys.*" For she wanted him to know that she was willing to stay; he was just to go on with his "explainings of those outlandish things."

Gert Petrus could hardly listen for joy. He kept his patient eyes on his mother's indomitable face. He distinctly saw it soften, little by little, and he saw wonder and understanding and surprise play across her hard, pinched features, like color in a kaleidoscope.

The lioness was bearded.

Every reserve the old grandmother had built up was swept away by the amazing flood tide of evidence. Once convinced, she was just as indomitable in defending the truth as she had been in opposing it. She quickly got to her feet at the close of the meeting.

"Why, Gert," she said excitedly, "why didn't you tell me about this? Your ranting was like the singing of a mosquito in the face of all this!"

Gert looked surprised. His mother's old dictatorial manner took a new trend.

"But, Gert," she said, her eyes sweeping over the faces of the few neighbors gathered there, "where are the Prinsloos, and the Lourens, and the Van Prys? Where are the Du Torts and the Du Prees? This building ought to be packed and crowded when truths as important as these are being preached. This is shameful. We must round up the rest of the neighbors. We must send pickaninnies everywhere, and force them to come." The old lioness was again roaring her supreme cry. But this time it was of a different tune.

Old *Vrou* de Beer's conversion was nine-days' wonder. It served to make everyone sober up and do a little investigating on his own. Everybody knew that she would not have capitulated if there had been nothing to this new belief that had sprung up among them like a mushroom. And she stood stanch and firm for her new faith till she died, battling to the very last; but this time it was for the good fight of faith."

John de Beer shot up tall and slim, like a gum tree by a drift. He was sober and dependable, and was Gert's standby and his joy. His mother's eyes followed him pridefully, for he was a good son, respectful, affectionate, and helpful to large and small.

Now his mother was especially solicitous, for her tall son was going away—going far to the south to school in a suburb of Cape Town. Peter Wessels had come and said that they must send the lad.

"You must make this John into a worker for God," Peter had said, gravely.

"What chance has he here? It's a new age, Gert Petrus, and the young people must be given their rightful chance in this world. The word must be preached. John will be a good worker."

"What must I do, Peter?" Gert had asked.

"Send him to our Union College. It's at Kenilworth, near Cape Town. He can meet all the big men, and he can associate with the Adventist young people. No place like it in Africa, Petrus."

"Then, I'll send him!" declared Gert excitedly. "John shall have his chance."

And so John went off to college. Cape Town was very far away in those days. It took several days of uncomfortable riding in the most primitive of steam cars to get there. He never forgot the morning he bade good-by to his mother. She clung to him, weeping wildly, as if she could not bear to tell him good-by. Perhaps she had a premonition that she would never look on his fair young face again—for she never did. She died only a short time after that. They buried people the same day they died. There was no embalming in those days, and the climate was heartless. John never saw his mother again.

Kenilworth! Union College! To John, every day was delightful and fascinating. Prof. E. B. Miller, of Battle Creek, Michigan, was principal. The work of Africa was growing! Every new attainment was a thrill. In Plumstead an orphanage was established, which later blossomed into a sanitarium, and many missionary nurses were trained there. And even though Claremont Union College was later moved to Spion Kop, near Ladysmith, Natal, and still later was moved to a country location at Somerset West, Cape Province, where it was renamed Helderberg College, old Union College still rouses nostalgic memories in the hearts of "old timers." For the Sentinel Publishing Company now occupies what was once College Hall. Some of the finest workers in South Africa were trained there.

So used had John been to the rolling veld, the loneliness which had dimensions, that the scenes of activity and the city noises excited his interest. He rode sometimes on the horsecars, and he told one of his friends, "This is certainly a modern world! What else can it be that man can invent? Surely the end of knowledge is at hand!"

His bright blue eyes took in the leisurely Victorian pace of life that people held at that time in old Cape Town. Long dresses swept the street. Men in tall hats and swallowtailed coats strutted up and down like peacocks. The grand "Parade" ground in front of the old fort was full of puddles when it rained. Even then it was the custom to sell everything under the sun on the two

70

market days every week. John used to wander about, among the tables piled and stacked with old books, cracked dishes, old clothes, and junk of all kinds. Today it is marked off as a perfect place for car parking—-but it was not so in John de Beer's school days. There were still leopards on Table Mountain and at night hyenas cried.

John felt thrilled, when he walked along Adderly Street, to realize that beneath the surface of the street still flowed the Platteklip Gorge, which filled the barrels of the Portuguese and Dutch navigators from the earliest days. Yet even then, the street was not the lovely thoroughfare it is today, smooth paved and with modern stores and offices. Automobiles whiz to and fro where once the slaves were driven up from ships and where the crack of the ox whip was heard. Where Hottentots brought wares to sell to the first few settlers, beautiful bazaars invite purchasers to buy merchandise never dreamed of in those faraway days.

The streets were full of the happy Cape Coloreds, selling flowers set in great tubs or driving swiftly along cobbled streets, their bouncing carts heaped high with vegetables and flowers.

John took his classes seriously. The dignified, bearded professors presiding over the classrooms inspired him with a zeal to learn and learn and learn. His clear young eyes took in everything. His heart was full to the bursting to go forth and spread the light of God. At last he was ready. His diploma and books were packed. He was eager to 11 go forth." By his side was a lovely, eager, brown-eyed wife, who was willing to undergo any hardship to help her John in his lifework.

The work was very hard to start in some parts of Africa, because of the gross heathenism that was difficult to penetrate. But among the Pondo people! What could be harder!

Little lights were springing up here and there like beacons on a dark, stormy night.

In May of 1894 Peter Wessels and A. Druillard, with five other brethren, penetrated into Matabeleland, and Solusi Mission was opened on a barren waste of sandy bushland interspersed with large stony *kopjes*.

Malamulo, Inyazura, Maranatha, Barotseland, and Rusangu missions were as yet unborn. But Pastors J. F. Wright and W. H. Branson made the long journey into east Pondoland to search for a place for a mission. They seemed to be hedged in on all sides. It was "No! no!" here, and "No! no!" there until the brethren were discouraged.

Some of the native people put red clay on their faces and dyed skins and coarse blankets red to wrap about themselves. They were called Red Kaffirs. Still others took white soil and made their faces a ghastly white. Some rubbed mud into their hair, pulling and pulling until the woolly kinks were straightened out and the mud, on drying around the hair, made a circlet all around their heads. A huge doughnut intricately beaded, pressed like a coronet over the muddy mess, and Eureka! the Pondo maiden had a most permanent hair-do, ready to be admired by all and sundry.

At last the brethren, rounding a breath-taking pass about a lovely mountain, came upon a most beautiful location, nestled in a fertile, grassy valley. But alas! The Salvation Army held this gem of a spot, and had for thirty-five years. It was perhaps fortunate, for Europeans were not permitted to buy land unless it had been held previously by other Europeans. It had originally belonged to Chief Mkuula of the Baca tribe.

The pastors felt impressed to make an offer for the beautiful mission site. To their surprise, the Salvation Army missionaries were willing to sell, for they said they had not had any success there whatsoever. Our brethren felt that this was the direct guidance of the Lord. So the three thousand acres of rolling veld and forests, streams and rich soil, was bought. Cancele Mission was born. You cannot say Cancele as the Xosa and Pondo and Griqua people roll it out. If you make a noise like an explosion of a wad of bubble gum for every *c*, you'll faintly approach the proper pronunciation.

Here to this isolated spot of primitive grandeur young John de Beer, son of Gert Petrus, and grandson of Johannes de Beer was called. Here he brought his bride around the perilous pass, with all their pots and kettles and bridal gifts. And her first little home to prettify and to delight in was a circular Zulu hut, made of mud and wattles, roofed with grass, and the floor smeared with cow dung.

Did her heart faint? and did she weep a little for the security and comfort of her father's house? Did she remember the immaculate rooms at Union College, with tall, airy windows and filmy white curtains? Did she think of the markets heaped with food of all kinds, and did she wonder just a little where their next meal would come from? If so, she did not let the matter rest too heavily on her heart, for she was young and gay and full of courage.

It wasn't a day before the small round hut began to look like home. The bed was decked with her pretty quilts, and shelves were made of packing boxes and curtained with bright calico. A little hut in the back was made into a "kitchen" of sorts, and was soon presided over by a "cook" who hardly knew how to boil water.

72

Never mind! He could carry water from the stream, and rake the dooryard and pound lime to put on the walls. He was useful too in searching for food in those harsh days before gardens were producing or crops were sown. Sometimes he'd appear triumphantly with a hard, ill-favored little pumpkin and a few edible leaves. Very often he would boil the corn that had been pounded in a native mortar. This they called samp.

Hostile looks were bent on the young intruders by white and black people alike. Pastors warned their church members against the "Advents." Natives looked askance at the activities there in their midst. Then, as if boycott and hostility were not enough that first year, a terrible drought swept like a scourge of fire throughout Pondoland. The corn withered and dried up before the ears were formed. Streams went dry and the grasses of the veld were burned a harsh, dull brown. Hunger stalked in the villages; babies sickened and died. Old people in fluttering rags and skins crept weakly about like half-dead slugs. Every day, every night, the drums kept up their endless tattoo—like little children beating on a closed door.

"Great Spirit! Mulungu! Tixo! are you angry? Why do you withhold the rains from our fields and gardens? See, our children are dying! Can you smell our sacrifices, Tixo? Hear us, hear us, Tixo! "

Little fires wreathed up everywhere while the drums beat out their monotonous staccato.

One day while John was opening new land with a span of oxen, in the hope that rains would bless his crops, a man came to him across the dry plowed ground.

"*Nkos*," he said, hesitantly, "*Nkos*, the people are dying. Death is walking in the villages. Other white people of the 'Sunday' churches have prayed, but no rains have come. The white man's God is angry, and the black man's god will not hear. The other white men have said it is your 'Saturday' God who is sending us this hunger. They tell us to stay away from you, for your God has no power to hear prayers. But now, we see the 'Sunday' God has no power. Our chief has said, 'Let us now try the Saturday God.' *Nkos*, will you come? Bring your *Nkosikazi* and she will pray too. We must have rain or we will all die."

Leaving a native helper with the oxen, John de Beer, tall and straight as an Indian, followed the messenger across the field to the little wattle-and-daub hut he called home. Bidding the young man wait, he and his young wife went into that little hut and closed the door. Together they knelt by the bed, and buried their faces in Mrs. de Beer's bright patchwork quilt.

"O God!" John literally groaned in spirit. "O God above! Now is our chance to reach the hearts of these people' O God' " Tears were raining down his checks now. "You hold the keys of things, Honor us this day, Fat-her, and bless this land with rain!"

Sobs shook his strong, young body, but as the two arose, they knew, yes, they knew surely, indubitably, that the God of the faithful would hear.

Together they walked across the dry veld to the kraal where the prayers were to be offered. But that day there was no talking, no laughter, no movement. Listless people, drained of hope, sat gaunt and sad in apathetic silence. They had hardly the strength to lift hopeless eyes to look at them as they passed by.

The old chief rose and greeted them soberly. The sky seemed brass. The sun glared down pitilessly on the seared and hard-baked earth. Babies with faces like little old men and with swollen bellies clung to their mothers with clawlike hands. It was a sight to melt a heart of stone.

John stood before this silent assemblage the first messenger of' hope to a hopeless people. His was the first voice to be raised in proclaiming the third angel's message to the Pondo people.

In the simplest words he could command he brought before them the peculiar truths that make our message so greatthe second coming of Christ, and the obligation of keeping the seventh-day Sabbath. Then in his kind, persuasive voice he gave a most wonderful sermon on the love of God and of His watchcare over His people.

"He loves you with an undying love," John said softly, looking down with great compassion on the pitiful sight before him. "He does not want you to die. Yet it is sin that keeps the Lord from answering prayers. Do you have sin in your hearts? Have you lied? Have you cheated? Have you stolen? Sometimes God has to bring us a great deal of trouble to make us think of great things. If you always had good crops, you would follow the drums, make beer, and dance. If death never came to the villages, how soon we would forget who gives us life! So the Father sometimes has to bring hard things to us to lead us back to a better way of living.

"Today, at this great *indaba*, you have asked me to pray for rain. But first I must ask you a question, before I pray. Will you pray to God to help you to live better lives? Will you leave off drinking beer, and following after witchcraft? God cannot bless a people who follow the devil."

Then John waited. Slowly the old grizzled chief arose, and addressed a few words to his people. They murmured assent. Then he turned to the young minister:

"The people say they would like to try your way, *Nkos*, Our way has failed."

"Jesus, our God, never fails if we keep our promises to Him!" cried John fervently, the light shining from his eyes. "Let us all kneel now, and let us all ask the great God to forgive our sins and cleanse our hearts. If we put ourselves, as little children, under His care, then we shall see that He will take care of us!"

God was very near to young John de Beer in that hour. He poured out his very heart in agony of soul before God. And the God of the prophet Elijah heard the young man's prayer, for hardly had the vast crowd dispersed toward their homes before the sky began to darken, and great black thunderheads tumbled over one another ominously, till the whole sky was black and angry. jagged lightning ripped the sky and the thunder rolled almost incessantly. Then it began to pour and pour. The hungry earth drank it in, and the dry creek beds sang again to the music of dimpling streams. The people danced for joy. Even through the drenching rain, people crept joyfully with gifts to the wattle-and-daub hut of the rainmaker; for so young Pastor de Beer was called by the grateful Pondo people. What did it matter if his grandfather's land was honeycombed with diamond mines? Why should he worry even though others were enriched with what might have been his? Here in Pondoland he found greater riches than ever were unearthed at Vooruitzight; for here at Cancele he found out that God will truly honor His children and that the prayer of a righteous man availeth much.

It rained there in thirsty Pondoland for almost a week, and every drop that fell was a living witness that God *does* hear the prayers of the "Saturday" people.

"Your God *does* hear," cried the old chief one morning when Pastor de Beer went near his village. His whole family were out busily planting maize and beans in the damp earth. "Do not go away, rainmaker!" he cried gaily, his old black face splintered with smiles. "Do not go away! Pondoland needs you!"

And so the hostility was turned to favor, and the grim boycott, to open-armed welcome. Because other mission societies had told the superstitious natives that it was the "Saturday" people who caused the drought, hardly a grain of food could they buy for love or money. Now that the "Saturday" people had brought the rain, there was a marked reversal in their attitude. Chickens, eggs, bananas, pumpkins, goats, sheep, and cattle were brought and offered to the rainmaker. Now everyone seemed eager that hunger should not walk on the new mission, and the people brought eagerly of their slender stores.

A large new tent traveled the long, long distance from Cape Town to Pondoland. It was transported over the tortuous passes of the Drakensberg Mountains by train and oxcart until, after many weeks, it came to the new missionaries at Cancele. It was put up, much to the native people's astonishment and admiration. The rainmaker had a house of cloth! A house of cloth that kept out the rain and shaded people from the sun! People came from far and near to see the marvel.

Then other church leaders began to make trouble. Some were vindictive enough to suggest that the villagers go pull down the tent and spoil young De Beer's work.

The old headman listened with deep amazement to their suggestion. Why did these worshipers of God despise the rainmaker? The rainmaker was their friend. Solemnly, he made his way to the space behind the big tent where Pastor John was making benches for the tent.

"The rainmaker has won a great battle over the other bulls of the kraal," he said solemnly. "Now, the other bulls are bellowing."

Young John stopped planing and wiped the fragrant red curls of wood from the smooth board.

"What do you mean, *Ubaba*?"

"The bulls, the enemies of the rainmaker, are bellowing. They hate the house of cloth." He repeated significantly. "*Nkos* must prepare for war."

Then the experience of godly Nehemiah came to John de Beer's mind. No time for controversy or debate.

"The work of God must be done," he told the chief. I have no time for quarrels or fights."

And so it was that in the face of great opposition, Cancele Mission slowly grew. A beautiful church rose on the spot where the tent had billowed and swirled in sunshine and rain. The timbers in the church were grown, cut, sawed, all right there on the mission. A new mission house rose by the untiring labors of Pastor de Beer and his willing helpers. But this was not so easy as it sounds.

Old Minah *Nkosi* is still alive and is a faithful Seventh-day Adventist. She comes every week to Cancele church and worships in peace and happiness. But it was not always so with her in her younger days. In the face of terrible persecution she took her stand for God under John de Beer's preaching. Her husband, a raw heathen, was mad with fury when she joined the baptismal class. He forbade her to go to church and above all, he told her she could never, never be baptized. Minah looked into his cold black face, frozen into lines of dreadful cruelty. She did not dare to answer back, but she knew she couldn't obey such a command. He might possess her body, but he could not own her soul. So secretly Minah went, even at odd times when her husband was in the fields, to study and learn at Pastor de Beer's. The day of the baptism was set, and Minah's name was on the wonderful list! She crept home, filled with deep joy that on the morrow she would be buried with her blessed Lord in baptism.

"My husband must not know of that baptizing! " she whispered. I think he will kill me if he hears!"

"No, he must not be told!" everyone whispered. "He is like the devil himself when he is angry.

But someone told him, and with a heart of stone and satanic craft, he waited. The next day he pretended to go to the mealie lands. Minah set out joyously to the baptism, a clean new cloth wrapped around her slender body. She saw the long procession off in the distance, making their way down to the river. Joy lent wings to her heels; she had only to pass this rough tool hut and she'd soon catch up!

But just then the bulky form of *Nkos*i, her husband, crossed her path. He held a cruel *sjambok* in his hand. Such a whip, made of the stiffest cowhide, can inflict horrible wounds. Slaves have died after such floggings. Towering above her he shouted, "Back, Minah, back, I say."

Minah turned to run, to elude him, but she caught her foot in the long grass by the edge of the path and fell. Even as she fell she heard the whistle of the descending whip, and felt the blood begin to trickle. Writhing to and fro in the grass, she could only shield her face from the terrible sjambok as it descended again and again, leaving her young brown back in blood-blackened ribbons. Then she fainted. When she awakened, her husband had gone and had taken her clothing with him. She crept to a house near at hand and borrowed an old ragged cloth. Then creeping, stumbling, weeping, and leaving a trail of blood, Minah someway got down to the stream. Pastor de Beer was aghast at the sight of her and would have put off the baptizing.

"You're hurt too badly, Minah," he said, "I'm afraid. Let's wait!"

"No, today. Now," she whispered, swaying a little as she stood there. "Tomorrow may be too—late."

So Minah, bruised, lacerated, and bleeding for the sake of the Lord Jesus, was baptized that day so long ago. Young Mrs. de Beer tenderly dressed her terrible wounds, and Minah went home to-she knew not what. But God was merciful. Her husband saw her patience, her childlike simplicity and grace. He saw with great amazement that she bore him no grudges, but went on trying to be sweet, even though he knew he had nearly killed her. Her love ultimately won him, till he too was buried in baptism, and died in the hope of the first resurrection. Minah still lives, and is an old, old woman. Her whole back is a mass of hard furrowed scars that she will bear with her to the grave.

Today, Cancele stands lush and beautiful—a living monument to the untiring labors of Pastor John de Beer. The whole mission is fenced. Fine cattle feast on the lush grasses, and water is piped from a living spring right to the mission, The little dairy turns out delicious butter, cream, and milk. Grapes hang in great bunches from long arbors. There is fruit in abundance, the result of the labors of Elder de Beer and others. The greatest need of all that South Bantu field is for church houses for the eager believers to meet in for worship. The churches at Queenstown and Lusikisiki are both far too small. Some companies of up to 150 members have to meet out of doors. Many of the churches are small and squalid, with just smeared cowdung floors. Yet out of this vast land and from these poor places will be translated into the new earth many a personwho will walk the golden streets. For it says that "the nations of them which are saved shall walk in the light" of that holy place.

"They shall hunger no more, neither thirst any more." Do you hear, poor Africa? "Neither shall the sun light on them, nor any heat." Your sun is pitiless, Africa. "For he that hath mercy on them shall lead them, even by the springs of water shall he guide them." He will guide you, too, Minah, and a whole throng of others who found God long ago in east Pondoland!

Jotham's Little Ewe Lamb

Jotham's Little Ewe Lamb

Vine Hall, one of the dormitories in the exclusive Sherwood-Condon Boarding School for girls, was the last word in luxury. The great ivy-mantled building, with deep porches and picture windows, stood at the top of a hill that sloped gently down to the edge of a beautiful lake. Rustic benches stood invitingly about, and farther down were a boathouse and a beach with every rich appointment known.

In the center of the lake was a tiny island, room for only a dozen or two to land and lounge about. There were a few trees there, and lush grass. Thoughtful hands had built a little grill and a rough table. Often parties of the girls were allowed to row to the island, to mill cocoa, scramble eggs, and roast potatoes at the little grill. Accustomed as they were to having all of these services performed for them, it was a "picnic" to do it themselves. Here they would shriek with laughter, spill the cocoa, burn the eggs and themselves, and talk later of their adventure for days on end.

Rosalee Hammond and Sybil Sayers were walking down the green hillside late on in early fall afternoon. Lines of discontentment furrowed the faces of both girls. Rosalee had a round face framed by corn-silk curls and a pleasingly plump figure. Sybil was tall, exceedingly slender, and dark to the point of swarthiness. School was out for the afternoon, and the girls, bored with books, had gone outside. Suddenly Sybil spoke.

"It's too cold to swim. Too windy for boating. I'm in no mood for tennis or croquet. What can we do?"

But Rosalee stood looking off at the town nestled in the valley below them, like a handful of dregs in the bottom of a green cup. Off to one side, on the hill opposite, they could see a small cottage surrounded by evergreens. A cheap car, looking like an explorative beetle, labored up the hillside road and stopped in front of the small house. Even from this distance they could see the door open and several children stream out.

"Haven't you often wondered, Sybil," Rosalee asked dreamily, "how people like that live? When we do go home, we seldom see dad or mother either. At least I don't. Mother's off to some club or meeting and father's off to ministerial councils, or playing polo, or golf, or something. The servants keep us washed and fed, but what's that? You could get that in an orphanage. I don't ever remember running out to meet dad, as those kids do." She pointed off to the gay party ascending the porch opposite, the father carrying the smallest one and the others tagging him—" He's supposed to be a minister, but he doesn't minister much to us. Not that I don't like the old dear," she added hastily. "But he just hasn't time."

Sybil curled her lips and bent a superior glance upon her friend.

"Why does *that* look attractive to you?" she sneered. "Not to me, thanks. I never relished 'slumming.'" ' Turning, she went back toward the great brick building and left Rosalee looking wistfully toward the happy family opposite. What did such people do? How could they be happy pinching and saving and matching pennies? In all her sheltered young life she had never voiced a desire that was not granted by an indulgent father and a proud mother. She had never known cold or hunger or misery.

Acting on an impulse, Rosalee started down toward the road. It was three hours until dinner. This was free time. Of course, they weren't supposed to leave the grounds, but—who'd know? who'd tell? She'd think up some excuse to investigate that family, if she had to fall down and pretend to sprain her ankle right at their very door.

Passing the lofty, arched gares, the girl came onto a narrow sidewalk, with grass growing in the cracks. Since the evening was chilly, she drew her smart green swagger coat a little tighter about her and unconsciously adjusted her beret. She could hear the voices now. And she was staring so concentratedly ahead that she caught the toe of her sports shoe on a protruding snag of sidewalk, and before she could catch herself, she had sprawled flat. Her desired sprawl had come quite uninvited. The knees of her sheer hose were torn, and so were her knees. Before she could rise, two of the older children scurried out to help her. Then she was in the house, guided there by the two loudly sympathizing children, and conveyed to a kitchen as clean as the inside of a china cup.

Something savory, smelling like tomato and onion, was simmering on the back of the stove. The baby, so lately crowing in her father's arms, no", stood unsteadily, grasping the sides of a gay, red splint-bottomed chair. She was regarding the visitor with wide brown eyes, dewy mouth ready to smile, her fuzzy head cocked sidewise like an inquisitive robin. Rosalee longed to take her into her arms. But Mrs. Lutes had appeared now with a tin tray full of first-aid supplies. Barbara, the rangy, ten-year-old girl, had a clean basin of water, and a fat cake of soap ready on a little stool.

Rosalee experienced feelings such as she had never felt before when plump Mrs. Lutes knelt and helped her to peel off the ruined stockings.

"You really got a bruise, dear," she said kindly, and Rosalee noted how vibrant with sympathy her loving voice was.

"I'll have to wash it, and it's going to hurt. There are gravel and sand in the wound. And Barby," she addressed her daughter, "run in and get a pair of my silk stockings out of the top drawer." Then turning to Rosalee she smiled. "They're not as nice as yours, but they'll do till you get back to the school."

"I'll bring them back tomorrow," promised Rosalee, secretly rejoicing in a legitimate excuse for another errand to this most interesting home.

Her knees neatly plastered, and sheathed in Mrs. Lutes' silk stockings, Rosalee reluctantly arose to go. Off in the breakfast nook, gay in red and white, with geraniums in the window, Rosalee saw some plum buns and a gingerbread cooling or-, a flat rack, its glossy brown crust looking like ambrosia. She could see Barby setting the dining table, and Bob carefully stowing his bat and ball in the corner, preparatory to washing for supper. If only just then Barbara came in.

"Mom," she said wistfully, "maybe Miss—Miss—"

"Rosalee," the girl supplied eagerly.

"Maybe Miss Rosalee can play the piano. We have a new one," she added proudly to Rosalee, "and I'm beginning lessons next week. Mom can play hymns. We like that so much, but we'd love to hear you. I went to a concert once and heard someone playing like waterfalls 'n birds singing. Can you do that?" Her little face was pointed with eagerness.

"Show me the piano," smiled the girl, filled with deep inward joy that her visit need not be terminated yet. At first she felt it was a situation where angels might fear to go. She had longed to "rush in," yet she feared "to tread." Now the ice was thawing and she seemed to begin to almost "belong." She sat down at the piano, thankful to the very depths of her soul for the years of piano and organ under real masters of music, whose discipline had been rigid in the extreme.

Looking around at the eager, sweet faces ranged about her, she began to play sweet melodious things—heartgripping melodies she knew they would understand and love—her fingers flying over the keys. She executed the trills and waterfalls and the tinkly runs up and down the keyboard, and was gratified to see Barby's delighted freckled face screwed up with an ecstatic smile. Mr. Lutes held the baby, and Mrs. Lutes came and went from the kitchen, where she was watching over supper. Bob came in, hair plastered, parted crookedly, with a distinct little-boy water line on his brown neck. He stared open-mouthed at her nimble fingers, looking again and again into her face with curious wonder and admiration. Strange that he should later attribute his amazing musical accomplishments to that vibrant joyful evening hour in his childhood home.

When Rosalee finally arose, she noted with secret glee that a place had been set for her at the table. Barby pulled her to the table.

"You sit next to me, see?" she said proudly, and Bobby gallantly pulled out her chair.

"We'll take you home after supper," Mr. Lutes added. "When we put the children to bed we often go for a walk if the weather is fair. It makes us feel as if we were sweethearts again."

Instantly the children raised a clamor to "go along," but were silenced by the father's upraised hand. Then a strange thing happened. Every head was bowed and Mr. Lutes began to thank God for the food that had been provided them. He thanked God for a good day, for dear children, and a new friend.

Rosalee stared at his earnest face and then at the brown-haired mother, her hand holding the baby's dimpled hands over the little face. It was all so sweet and sacred that Rosalee wished she need not go back to the cold, impersonal grandeur of the boarding school. True, on Sundays "grace" was said at the gleaming, perfectly appointed tables, on the occasion of a visiting minister, but it was all very cold and impersonal. It was as if God were some august, austere, vindictive Being, who seemed only to want laud and appeasement. The God of this family must be different, for here in the lamplit hour He seemed very near. Almost as if He lived here—"Perhaps He does," she thought.

Then Mrs. Lutes lifted the cover to the great blue tureen, and began ladling soup. The smell was tantalizing and the dish of crisp crackers went around.

Bobby crumbed his crackers in his soup and ate with the hungry, unconscious gusto of a small boy. But Barbara narrowly watched the dainty manners of the guest and imitated adorably.

Then the gingerbread was brought in, the rich-textured, plushy squares exuding a most delightful fragrance. Mrs. Lutes heaped each one generously with whipped cream and topped it with a cherry before the servings were passed around.

Later, in the big dining room, Rosalee's friends chided her in well-bred tones for her lack of appetite. "It can't be your health," commented Sybil, languidly nibbling an olive. "You look as if you'd had a long, brisk ,k,alk in the cold air."

84

Yes, thought Rosalee, there was the brisk walk, and there was the feeling of superb health. But who could eat these pallid slices of roast lamb, or the fish course, or these parsley potatoes and steamed carrots, almost stamped with institutional flavor, when one was full of real vegetable soup, rich and odorous Mexican rice, hot rolls dripping with butter, and gingerbread? Rosalee smacked her lips at the memory.

Rosalee's visits to the Lutes became so frequent that the children spied her often and ran to meet her. One day they brought the baby, who held up dimpled arms and crowed with delight when Rosalee took her into her loving arms.

On a Friday afternoon soon after this, Rosalee had her first real surprise. She had slipped over to the little bungalow while her chums were playing bridge. So far, she had not even roused an inkling of curiosity as to her ramblings.

But this was the first Friday afternoon she had ever gone over there. The comfortable little home rang with activity as she went up the walk. What could be happening? She heard, "Mom, come and give me a towel!" from the bathroom, and, "Mom, the bread's brown," from the kitchen. Then, "Barby, bring Mommie the soap. There's a dear," from somewhere else. It was all very strange but as harmonious as a symphony. It seemed to blend into the wondrous vibrant chords of a home life she had never known nor seen. They were getting ready for something. What was it? Where were they going, or who was coming, or what?

As the visitor mounted the kitchen steps familiarly, Barbara spied her first.

"Oh, come in, Miss Rosalee!" she cried with delight. "We're getting ready for Sabbath, and this is a special day, for Teeny's coming home."

The little girl's face glowed with joy as she plunged her small arms into the dishwater.

"Who's Teeny?" asked Rosalee, curiously, "and what's the Sabbath?"

Bobby came in just then with his father's shoes and the blackening box.

"Sabbath?" he laughed. "Why, Miss Rosalee, tomorrow's Sabbath. We get ready for it every Friday. We call Friday prep'ration day, 'cause mom prep'rations the food and we prep'ration the baths and the house and shoes and clothes. Can't work on Sabbath, see?" and he trudged on through the kitchen to the back porch as if his duty was done.

Rosalee stared at him, and then at Barbara. Just then Mrs. Lutes came in, with the rosy baby wrapped in a fluffy towel. She greeted Rosalee warmly, then sat down to dress the little bundle of sweetness.

"Let *me* dress her, please," begged the girl. "You do something else, and tell me who Teeny is and what is a *Sabbath!*"

Mrs. Lutes laughed and handed the willing baby over to Rosalee's eager arms. The tiny garments were folded neatly on the chair.

"Well, I'll tell you a little while I'm mixing up this potato salad." She got a bottle of mayonnaise out of the refrigerator and a pan of cold boiled potatoes and several boiled eggs. Deftly her fingers diced and sliced and minced and tossed until a most delightful concoction was prepared. While she worked she talked, and Rosalee thrilled at the vibrancy of her rich voice.

"Why, Teeny is our daughter," she said sweetly. "She's about your age and has been away to college. Our church has a college up near the lake, and we sent her there. Now, you asked about the Sabbath. You see, Rosalee, most of the world worships God on Sunday, but we worship on

Saturday, because that is the day God told us to keep, and that is the day that Jesus kept."

Rosalee nodded impatiently. "I never heard of such a thing!" she declared. "Are you Jews? Don't you know that the old Jewish Sabbath was changed or something? My father is a bishop, and it seems as if I've heard him say something like that. Maybe you never read about it in history."

Mrs. Lutes gave a ringing laugh, and then led the girl to the built-in bookcases filling one whole wall in the living room.

"Look!" she said, pointing to row after row of histories. Rosalee got a fleeting glimpse of Macaulay, Robinson, Beard, Shapiro, Gibbon, D'Aubigne, and a dozen others.

"My husband is a student of history. He doesn't take anybody's word for anything. He runs everything down and proves everything. Then when he finds out that he is absolutely right beyond the shadow of any doubt, that's what he *does*. That's why we keep Saturday instead of Sunday."

"Why, I never heard of such a thing," Rosalee gasped. "I wonder if my father ever heard of it. He's president of one of the biggest theological seminaries in the country. There's a girls' school near there where he wants me to teach when I finish this year, but—"

"But what, dear," Mrs. Lutes pursued. She had packed the potato salad into a refrigerator dish and was now taking a casserole of baked beans from the oven.

"What is in the back of your mind?" she turned and smiled at the girl.

"Why, I don't want to leave rill I find out more about this. Is it wrong to keep Sunday? Why do you have to keep *Saturday*? What's the difference, anyway? Isn't one day as good as another?"

Just then Mr. Lutes came in. "What's this?" he asked pleasantly. "Is our friend Rosalee wanting to know why we keep Saturday? Well, stay for supper and we'll tell you a little, but it's a long story. I'm taking the car and going to the station to meet Teeny. You put supper on, Mother, while I'm gone. I'll be back in a Jiffy."

"Oh, let me help," begged Rosalee. "You know, I've never been in a *home* before. At our house the cooks and the maids do it all. I just love to try some things!"

"Barby is setting the table," Mrs. Lutes answered. "You help me make sandwich spread. Teeny loves a sandwich supper on Friday night. We have cocoa, raspberry pie, and bread, butter, and lettuce. We make our own sandwiches. It's fun."

"What can I do then?" Rosalee asked eagerly, while Mrs. Lutes tied a pretty apron around her.

"Here are six boiled eggs and some pimento and onion. Mix them all together, and grate some of this cheese with it. Teeny loves it with rye bread. Here's the mayonnaise. Thin it with some milk. I'll finish the egg savory."

"Oh, this is delightful," Rosalee decided as she shelled the boiled eggs and awkwardly minced onion. "Oh, if home were only like this!" Black and white checkered linoleum, red and white curtains. And best of all-love. And exchanging recipes with this good woman filled her heart to overflowing.

" What's egg savory?" she asked interestedly.

"See these tomatoes?" asked Mrs. Lutes. "I first browned an onion and then put a can of tomatoes in it. It has been cooking slowly for a half hour. That's the secret. Cook it slowly for a long time. Then add six beaten eggs— so," and she deftly emptied the eggs into the bubbling tomato and began to stir vigorously. "It's almost done now, and I am glad, for here they come!"

The whole family were soon ranged around the table, and after the blessing, they all laughingly made sandwiches. Teeny was Ernestine, a sweet brown-eyed girl with a heart-shaped face, who seemed to be everyone's delight. She was cordial to Rosalee, and the girl loved her on the spot.

"Now, you asked about this Sundaykeeping business," began Mr. Lutes. "I can't tell you much, for we must get you back to Vine Hall by seven o'clock. We don't want you to get into any kind of trouble because of us. But here is just a starter: "The true followers of Christ kept the Sabbath for two hundred years after the birth of Christ."

Rosalee gasped.

"Why, I thought it was nailed to the cross! I'm sure I've heard my father preach it that way on Easter Sunday many times. He made it sound so lovely— that we had entered a new dispensation and that Sunday should be spelled

"S-o-n-d-a-y," because God's only-begotten Son arose on that day."

"Rosalee, I'm sorry to tell you, but many of these socalled 'beautiful theories' have no basis of truth at all. Read your church history and you will find that the idea of worshiping on Sunday came in gradually. Constantine's law, in A.D. 321, first made it a legal rest day, and the

Roman Church forbade the people's keeping of the Sabbath and promoted the observance of "the venerable day of the Sun" instead. But, Rosalee, *all through the ages* the Sabbath has never been lost. There have always been people who refused to 'sell out' to paganism."

"But what difference does it make?" pursued the girl earnestly. "Is God so particular as all that?"

"When is your birthday, Rosalee?" Ernestine asked quietly.

"Why, May 28," she answered, mystified.

"How would you like for people to come and change it arbitrarily to May 29 or May 30? Isn't one day as good as another? "

"B-but that wouldn't be my birthday!" protested Rosalee. "They couldn't do that'"

"That's why they can't change the Sabbath," Ernestine answered immediately. "It's the birthday of the world. They can't change it really, for then it wouldn't be the actual birthday, celebrated since the dawn of creation. just calling Sunday Sabbath doesn't make it so, does it?"

Before Rosalee could reply, Mr. Lutes looked at the clock and whistled softly. "Come, Teeny," he cried, "we must hurry to get Rosalee home! It's ten till seven!"

And so the weeks went by, and little by little Rosalee began to learn the truth about the real things of life.

Every hour she could spare she spent on such all absorbing things. The soon coming of Jesus terrified her until she saw how the whole Lutes family longed for that blessed day.

"Look how old Granny Smith suffers from arthritis," Mrs. Lutes pointed out. "The Bible says that in the new earth the inhabitants will never say, 'I am sick.' Granny Smith will possess glorious youth over there."

Then little Barby piped up eagerly, "I'm glad no one will cry in the new earth. 'Cause when little Wanda falls down and gets hurt, I just cry too. Seems so awful to hear babies cry."

"I'll like it 'cause the wild animals'll be tame," contributed Bobby. "I learned in school last week that 'the wolf also shall dwell with the lamb, and the leopard shall lie down with the kid; and the calf and the young lion and the fatting together; and a little child shall lead them.' I learned that in Bible class. We learn a mem'ry verse 'most every day. I'm glad too, for I want to be a preacher if Jesus doesn't come afore I'm grown up."

Having delivered himself of this long speech, Bobby took a little motorcar from his grubby pocket and began to emit explosive sounds from his small mouth, running his car up and down the blocks on the checkered linoleum, as carefree and happy as if he had not already imbibed some of the truest philosophies of an earth-bound life.

One Sabbath the family had a picnic off in the woods bordering the lake next to the college estate. Rosalee ate a hurried dinner, and then hastened to the place where the Lutes said they would be. Sybil and her other friends had long since given Rosalee up in disgust. They were too self-centered to be very curious, and dubbed her a bookworm, "the saint," and "Johanna Burroughs" when she read books, the Bible, and tramped often in the woods, bringing home wild flowers and bright leaves.

Then, scurrying through the woods on that day, she soon spied the family sitting on blankets by the bright waters of the lake. In a minute she was joyfully ensconced in the midst of the happy party. Mr. Lutes was reading from a book titled *The Great Controversy*, about a time he called the "time of trouble." When Rosalee asked for an explanation, the whole family eagerly joined in to explain.

"That's just before Jesus comes," put in Barbara. "The wicked people will be mad at the good, and will try to kill them."

"Why, how do you know?" asked Rosalee. "Don't tell me *that's* in the Bible too!"

"Why, yes," replied Mr. Lutes, and he turned in his Bible to Daniel 12: 1 and read it to the girl. The family group all kept still, even the children, while the father talked in his quiet, assured voice. Rosalee drank it in eagerly.

"Why, I never heard of such a thing!" she exclaimed. "Here I am, a *minister's* daughter, and sent to a denominational school, and I don't know as much about the Bible and prophecy as Bobby and Barbara."

"Course not," agreed Bobby sagely. "We've always gone to church and Sabbath school, and I mean, we *learn* it. We have to, and we want to. Our teacher really makes it interesting. You oughta hear her."

"Yes, and I just feel *sorry* for kids who don't *know* the coming of Jesus is so near. It just makes me so glad to think about it every time our singing band goes to the Children's Hospital. There are children there who have never walked or played in their whole lives. It's awful. I just love to sing, "Tis almost time for the Lord to come, I hear the people say.' The sick children like to hear it too.

Meanwhile the Right Reverend Doctor Hammond, Rosalee's father, had arrived at the college to have a brief visit with his young daughter between important committee meetings. Prof. Anna Colbern, head mistress, and Dr. Agnes Warbert, hovered anxiously over him while he paced up and down the reception room waiting for them to find the girl. Emissaries were sent hither, thither, and yon, scouring the estate for the missing girl. It was Sybil who found her.

"Who are those people?" she asked distastefully as they walked away from the group.

Rosalee was crushed and ashamed of Sybil's sneering patronage when she tried to introduce her friends.

"Really," Sybil said loftily, "so—Rosalee's been *slumming* again."

"No," protested the girl with scarlet cheeks. "My friends aren't that kind." There was cold fury in her voice that augured no good for Sybil at a later settlement, but the girl only smiled haughtily.

"Meanwhile Dr. Hammond is waiting most impatiently, and has been for more than half an hour. The dean is disturbed and Prexy is on needles and pins. Are you coming, or aren't you?"

With hardly a glance at the Lutes family, who were standing to bid good-by to Rosalee, Sybil walked away. Rosalee bade them all a loving good-by.

"The lunch was wonderful, and Bible study was the best ever. Did you say I could borrow this book? I want to read it."

So with a much-thumbed copy of *The Great Controversy*, Rosalee hurried after Sybil, and the two ran up the steps of Vine Hall. Dr. Hammond arose when she came in, red-cheeked, wind blown, and beautiful.

In her heart she was wondering whether to tell him yet about all the new things she had learned. Surely he would see the logic and the cleverness of the whole argument, when it was once presented, if she did it right, but today did not seem auspicious. So she tossed the book over onto the couch and went respectfully up to her distinguished father.

"O Father," she cried softly. "So good of you to come! And I'm sorry I wasn't here. I was out in the woods, reading and studying."

The somewhat pompous features of the aristocratic churchman relaxed at the sight of the vivid face of his young daughter. There was something sweet shining there—as if candies were lighted behind her dark eyes.

He looked at his wrist watch and cleared his throat uneasily.

"It's three o'clock, Rosalee. Go get slicked up a little, child. We have time to run over to town to pick you up a frock or two. Perhaps a hat, and shoes for your dainty feet," he added, looking over the lovely girl with fond appraisal. He was surprised to see a cloud come over her pretty eyes.

"Oh, no, not today, Daddy," she said a bit too hastily. "Not today. Really, I don't need a thing. Let's just sit and talk."

"This is strange indeed," laughed her father jovially. "Why, usually a daughter of mine never has a thing to wear, to hear her talk. Now, here's one who *doesn't want* a frock. What's the matter, Rosy? Sick?"

"No, Daddy," she replied, parrying for time. "I just don't see you often, and I want to sit and talk to you awhile. You see, there are some questions I'd like to ask you."

The Reverend Jotham Hammond, wide of girth, puffy cheeked, and many-chinned, leaned back jovially in the great stuffed chair with a self-satisfied air. He had a fashionable church of contented people; a proud, dressy wife who was an asset in every way; and two beautiful daughters and three grandchildren. This one ewe lamb was the secret delight of his heart and soul. She had taken to schooling as a fish takes to water. She hadn't been overly crazy over boys. Now, in Jessica's day, the whole house had been run over with bold sheiks who invaded every corner of the great house. He hadn't liked it—he hadn't had any privacy. The ring-a-ling-rat-a-tat-tat of jazz on phonograph, radio, and piano had penetrated everywhere, till he often had seized his hat and gone to his club for privacy, rest, and quiet. It had been a relief when Jessica had chosen one of the "gang," thrown a big church wedding, and gone into lavish matronhood. But Rosalee—Rosalee—the little darling, so soft, cuddly, and cute even from little-girl days, had pulled on his proud heartstrings in a special way.

Awakened from his pleasant paternal reverie, Dr. Hammond smiled placidly and tumbled Rosalee's curls.

"What's troubling my girl?" he inquired pleasantly. "If it's geometry or trigonometry, don't bother to ask, for I've forgotten more than I've ever learned."

He leaned back in the chair, and Rosalee leaned forward in hers, and looked at her father's face curiously. He seemed so satisfied-so sure of himself, and so solid, Yet in her heart she realized that home had never been the gay, loving, intimate place she had found the Lutes's home to be. There were never picnics in the woods or sandwiches toasted over a grill in the back yard. The kitchen at home wasn't a gathering place where wounds were bandaged, hurts were kissed, and babies were fed.

"Daddy, what is the 'time of trouble'?" she asked softly, the candles lighted behind her dark eyes.

Her father's eyes opened sharply, and he sat up suddenly.

"The *time* of *what*?" he asked sharply.

"The 'time of trouble,' Daddy. I read it in the book of Daniel. Look, here's a Bible. Let me read it to you."

She went and got a little Bible that Mrs. Lutes had given her and turned eagerly to the place they had been reading from that afternoon. She had not been able to stay to have it fully explained. Surely, her father, a bishop, a president of a seminary, would know as much as the Lutes. They were laity,' according to her father's often-repeated allusion to those not of the 'cloth.'

" 'And at that time shall Michael stand up,' she began to read in her clear, warm voice, " 'the great prince which standeth for the children of thy people: and there shall be a time of trouble, such as never was since there was a nation even to that same time: and at that time thy people shall be delivered, every one that shall be found written in the book.

" 'And many of them that sleep in the dust of the earth shall awake, some to everlasting life, and some to shame and everlasting contempt.'"

"There!" she said, smiling, looking at her amazed father, "what do you make of that? I read that only today." Her father was quite without speech for a long moment. He gazed fixedly at the face of this younger child of his, his face growing to an embarrassed red.

"*Rosalee*!" he exclaimed, "what in the *world* are you reading the Bible for? It's—it's, why—it's preposterous! It isn't natural. No young girl can understand it at all."

Rosalee was naivete itself.

"Daddy, only two weeks ago I was at home, you remember, and went to church with you. I distinctly remember your saying in your sermon that the Bible is a grand old book, and we would all be better and happier if we read some in it *every* day. Why did you say *that*, Daddy? "

"Yes, my girl," he argued, hotly, "but I didn't mean young girls like you. Anyway, if you *do* read it, why don't you read the Gospels? They're so easy that a *babe* could understand."

"Isn't it good, Daddy, for girls like me to be better and happier? If reading the Bible will bring such a result id, I want to read it. Anyway, Daddy, I have been as you said reading the Gospel of St. Matthew. Listen here to what I read today. It is in Matthew 24."

Rosalee turned the pages eagerly until she found her place and began to read from Matthew 24:3: 'And as be sat upon the mount of Olives, the disciples came unto him privately, saying, Tell us, when shall these things be? and what shall be the sign of thy coming, and of the end of the world?'

"There! Daddy," Rosalee cried, the tears streaming down her face, "why have you *never* told me about the end of the world or the second coming of Jesus, or the time of trouble? How can I get ready if I don't know about it? O Daddy, Daddy! there's so much I don't know."

"Why, Rosalee baby, you're all stirred up about nothing. Don't worry about the second coming. That will not happen in our day. Things are going along just as they have since the beginning—why, the same old sun shines on us as shone on Adam and Noah, and Jesus and St. Paul. Don't worry about *that*. Just live and be happy. Jessica never worries about such things! Don't trouble your pretty head! We don't even preach the second coming any more. Our church founders don't even believe it."

Real distress was in Jotham Hammond's voice. He took his handkerchief and tried to dry the girl's eyes.

"Listen, Daddy," Rosalee said in a tiny voice. She'd found another place in the Bible, her father noted with alarm. Why, was the girl crazy? What ever got her off on this tangent?

"This is 2 Peter 3:3, 4, Daddy," said the girl. She was secretly elated at her father's argument, for she had raised exactly the same objection that very day, and Mr. Lutes had answered with this very text. It had silenced her, and it would silence her proud father.

" 'Knowing this first, that there shall come *in the last days* scoffers, walking after their own lusts, and saying, Where is the promise of his coming? for since the fathers fell asleep, all things continue as they were from the beginning of the creation.' Listen, Daddy, you said the church founders didn't believe it. You've spoken time and again about Moody and what a wonderful man he was. Last week I found a book about him written by his son. Do you know what it said? 'My father believed in the second coming, and *taught* it.' I was astonished at that, Daddy. I began to wonder about the 'second coming.'"

"Then the other day in hymnody class, we were studying the songs of Charles Wesley. He believed in the I second coming' too. Oh, here's a hymnbook right here on the table. Let me show you!"

And Rosalee rapidly turned to a song.

"The name of this is 'Lo, He cornes.' Read it, Daddy, or shall I read it to you? Listen:

> " 'Lo! He comes, with clouds descending,
> Once for favored sinners slain;

93

Countless angels, Him attending,
    Swell the triumph of His train.
Hallelujah!
    Jesus comes, and comes to reign.'

"That awakened my curiosity. I looked up other songs of Charles Wesley, and be mentions the second coming several times. If the Wesleys and Dwight L. Moody believed in it, why shouldn't we? Weren't *they* founders?"

Jotham Hammond was so confused by the eloquence of his young daughter that be hardly knew whether to be proud or angry. Then he decided to try to calm her down and temporize, and put her questions off.

"Wait, wait, Rosy!" he laughed, though he was inwardly quaking. "You're getting a little too eloquent. If you keep up like this you'll get your father's job, for you'll be a better preacher than I am if I don't watch out. Come now, get your hat. Let's run in to town and pick you up a few things."

But Rosalee sat still and regarded her father soberly. "No, Daddy," she said quietly, "I don't want to go. Today is Sabbath, Daddy."

It seemed as if a bomb had exploded in the quiet room. For then it was that the Reverend Hammond moved faster than he had moved for many months. He leaped to his feet and seized the girl roughly by the shoulders.

"Rosalee," he cried, "where have you been? Who has poisoned your young mind? Seventh-day Adventists, I'll wager you. Rosy, *do* you know any Seventh-day Adventists? Have you been around them or have you been reading their diabolical books? Have you, I say?"

The girl raised her honest brown eyes to her father's face. She seemed quite unperturbed.

"Yes, Daddy. They're wonderful people. I've been studying with them for six months. I've tried harder than ever to be a good girl. I've learned to know and love the Bible. Daddy, you mentioned Jessica. Do you want me to be like her? Why, she smokes and drinks, and hangs out at the worst roadhouses. Her name has been linked lately with Dopey Thompson, and you know he's no good. She hardly sees her own children. Daddy, that's not the way a home should be run. There ought to be love and family life there. The children have a right to *know* their father and mother. There should be family life. That, to my mind, is the most wonderful thing in this old world."

Jotham Hammond sat before his young daughter as weak as if he had had a long illness. He could not seem to gather his thoughts together. In all his successful, satisfied life he had never been at such a loss for words. He opened his mouth to answer her, then closed it again.

94

Back in his mind he could not help admiring his young daughter, but this foolishness must stop. These Adventists were troublemakers, getting in where all was well and spoiling everything. Proselytizing. He had lost several influential members to them when their evangelistic meetings were held too close to his pastorate. And they'd never come back. He had stopped in to see them and had gotten into no end of difficulty, what with their quoting texts of Scripture and raising all sorts of questions he hadn't been able to answer at the moment. But Rosalee—Rosalee, his little ewe lamb. He must stop this at all costs.

"Now, listen, Rosy," he said, a trifle too patronizingly, you must trust father. I've been preaching more years than you are old. What could a girl like you know about these intricate questions of theology? Let *me* handle such things, my dear girl, and don't trouble your little head about such tiresome matters."

Rosalee said nothing—merely looked at her father, biting her red lips with her sharp white teeth. Why did father treat her as if she were a baby? She was old enough to graduate from college. Couldn't she choose her belief? Couldn't she act according to the dictates of her conscience?

She said no more—perhaps realizing the futility of the situation. Her father continued to reassure her in a loud voice, which lacked the quality of sincerity she listened vainly to hear. She noted too, with a sinking heart, that he couldn't meet her eyes but did much back and shoulder patting and hastily betook himself off.

Rosalee watched him go away. The night was gathering—darkness was closing in. It was a free evening—no study hour, and two hours till dinner. She stood irresolutely before the arched window, looking out on the dimming campus. The Luteses! She *must* see them. Acting on an impulse, she snatched up her red coat and beret, and let herself out of the door in a trice. Even though it was nearly dark, her feet knew the way—and it was only a few minutes until she was there. She was welcomed as usual, and there were guests. Two young men rose from their chairs when she entered the room, rosy and wind blown. Mr. Lutes made the introductions, for Mrs. Lutes was in the kitchen. She could hear the whir of the egg beater and smell the tantalizing aroma of supper cooking.

"Miss Hammond, this is my younger brother, Jack Lutes, home from college for the weekend. He just ran in to see us awhile this evening. This is Harry Collins, his roommate. He's a premedic. Hopes to be a regular sawbones someday.

"Jack and Harry, Rosalee, as we call her, is in the Sherwood-Condon college here. She graduates from the teacher's course in two weeks."

Rosalee found her hand grasped firmly by Jack Lutes, and his dark-brown eyes were upon her. She looked up into a good face, a strong and handsome face, in which goodness seemed to predominate. There were earnestness, merriment, and sincerity in the eyes. The full mouth seemed ready to smile or laugh, but it didn't seem incongruous to believe that he would pray too. The three waves in his combed-back hair did not look effeminate. They seemed to be in keeping with the expression on his face.

Harry seized her hand easily, his blue eyes full of appreciation of her beauty, but with nothing of the repulsive familiarity that Rosalee hated in Jessica's crowd of pleasure seekers.

"I am glad to know you, Miss Rosalee," Jack had said quietly. "The folks wrote and told me about you, and I'd hoped I'd meet you on this trip home. I graduate this year too, from theology."

"Me too," chimed in Harry eagerly. "So glad to meet you. Jim Lutes was just telling us that you're interested in prophecy. It's a great subject. I am taking a class in it this year myself—Prophecies of Jesus. It's just wonderful. We hate to see that class end. Of course Professor Jones is an excellent teacher, so spiritual and sympathetic."

They all sat down, and conversation seemed to develop spontaneously. Rosalee noted no restraint, no shady phrases with hidden meanings, no smirking laughter, but everything was frank and cheerful. Whenever she looked up she saw Jack's brown eyes upon her. It wasn't long until she learned that Harry was Teeny's best friend, and they had high hopes of going to the mission field when he finished medicine. Their enthusiasm stirred something deep within her.

"I have an uncle in Africa," Harry confided to her eagerly. "Every one of his letters is a challenge. Those mud villages, that leprosy, those ulcers, the diseases, and the witch doctors make me feel as if I can't wait to go where the need is so great."

"Oh, oh," protested Rosalee, with a shudder. "And you'd go there? You'd take Teeny? There are all kinds of dangers. I know, for I've read father's mission reports many times. In the atlas many of those countries are definitely designated as 'unhealthful for white people' ! "

It was Jack who answered her then, a light smoldering behind his dark eyes.

Miss Rosalee," he asked quietly, "do you think that when Jesus said, 'Go ye therefore, and teach all nations,' He meant for them to leave out Africa? There are old records which say that the apostle Matthew penetrated far into Africa, preaching the gospel, and died a martyr's death there. Thomas is supposed to have gone to India, and that is even worse than some parts of Africa. Peter told Christ, on the eve of His crucifixion, 'I am ready to go with thee, both into prison and to death.' That is how I feel. If God calls me to some dark land, I must say, 'Here am 1, Lord, send me.'"

Just then Mrs. Lutes called them all to supper, and included Rosalee in her general greeting. "You too, Rosalee dear. See? It's only six. I hurried supper so you could eat with us. Rosalee is Just like one of the family now," she said as they gathered around the table.

Jack sat just opposite her, and when the blessing was offered, she was thrilled to hear him give it in his quiet voice. The serenity and love of this lamplit home seemed beautiful, fitting, and proper. How different from the blaring music of juke boxes, heavily painted lips, dresses with plunging necklines, hard, glittering eyes, and raucous laughter met with so frequently in Jessica's crowd.

Africa? India? sores? heathenism? witch doctors? fevers? chills? Perhaps a lonely grave gashed out of a harsh hillside? All of these ran through the girl's subconscious mind as the meal went on happily. Scrambled eggs on toast, tall glasses of cold milk, sliced tomatoes, blueberry muffins, cottage cheese, and applesauce. Simple, yet delightful.

Africa? India? went tier truant thoughts again. Africa—why, if God wanted her there, she'd go! Better Africa, with its harsh, arid, rocky hillsides, or steaming, humid India than the whole procession of "high-class" night clubs, flasks, cigarettes, and obscene dances. They were worlds apart. One was of one world, and one of another. She knew now the path she would take.

All accompanied her home, except Mrs. Lutes and the smaller children. When Jack told her good-by, there at the great arched gate, he waited till the last, and lingered a moment after the others had turned to go.

"May I write to you, Miss Rosalee?" he asked quietly. "Tonight I was impressed by your—well—perhaps I might say, your interest in greater things. Maybe I could help you. I'm glad my brother Jim and Dora and the rest are near at hand. But school is soon out. You'll be going home—"

"Yes, and I have an appointment to teach in the school near our home. My father is on the board. I'm to teach English rhetoric."

"Will you let me write to you, then?" he repeated. "I'm going into a State conference in the South as a ministerial intern. I go in two weeks. Someway, I don't want to lose you! "

Rosalee looked up into his face, there in the moonlight, and inwardly agreed with her thumping heart that here was the nicest, yes, the very nicest young man she had ever met in her whole life.

"Yes, I'll be glad to write to you," she answered breathlessly, and after a brief handshake she ran up the steps of Vine Hall and to her room, missing supper there entirely. She wanted to think. She would lose the magic of that wonderful hour in the cold impersonality of the Vine Hall dining room.

She hung up her coat and put her beret away, then turned and looked at herself in the mirror. She looked like a stranger, even to herself. She looked at her reflection critically, as *he* might have looked at her tonight. Her hair was in tiny curly, fly-away tendrils all around her brow as if she were a little child, just in, rosy from play. Her cheeks were red, and her full lips were parted with the joy of just living—real, honest living.

"He said he didn't want to lose me," she whispered to herself. "He said he would follow Jesus to prison and to death—and, oh—I would—I would too!" She covered her face with her hands and stood for a long time—so.

Then she took her Bible and looked up the word *prison* in the concordance. After a long search she found the text she was looking for in the Gospel of Luke. Then she sat down and read of that night of trial, agony, and terror; of Peter's bold declaration and his later disgraceful denials. Yet the serenity and calm of the Saviour through all the insidious wickedness, through the lies, plots, and treachery was like a golden thread that brightened the whole tapestry. "The Saviour of the world," she whispered, 1. when I say, 'I will follow Thee to prison and to death,' I *mean* it. The cock may crow ten thousand times, yet I will never deny Thee!" And she never did. Never.

On the next Tuesday a letter came to her from her father. She broke the seal with trembling fingers. She had a premonition that it contained something unpleasant and discouraging.

"I'm sorry, my daughter," he had written, "I've had to write the school authorities there to forbid your visiting or communicating in any way with anyone in the village for the remaining week and a half of school. I've had to make this move because your belief is being undermined and your life is being ruined by conscienceless people. Now, do not become rebellious, for I will only clamp down all the harder. I'm determined to get this foolishness about 'second comings,' 'times of trouble,' and

'Sabbath' days out of your silly mind. Let us
old theologians worry about such complicated,
questionable doctrines. It isn't for *you* to worry
about, certainly. So be a good girl, and drop your
low-class friends and unsavory friendships. It
isn't wholesome or natural for a young girl to get
all stirred up like that. Mother sends her love.
She'd write, but she's going to Mrs. Prentiss's
for bridge.

    "Lovingly,
    "FATHER."

The words blurred, as her eyes filled and spilled over with tears. Then she looked up, a glint of anger in her eyes. Low-class friends, unsavory friendships, indeed! How could she give them up? Where could she go? There was no path back!

She ran up to her room and wrote a hasty note to her friends. The page was blotted with tears.

"I'm *so* sorry I can't come, but Annette will
bring you this letter. I'll send her to get your
answer tomorrow. I love you all so much I won't,
I can't, I'll never forget you or give you up.
I won't give up my faith either. Is there an
Adventist church near Harrington Heights? I want
to attend, and I want to be baptized. My father
can't be conscience for me, and I must do what God
tells me to do.

    "Lovingly,
    "ROSALEE."

Then she ran out in the hall and called the little maid who was polishing the floor, and gave her the letter. The girl tucked It In her pocket and disappeared.

Rosalee knew the girl would do anything for her. She had found out that Annette was the sole support of her family. Her father was dead and her mother was frail. Many of Rosalee's slightly worn frocks, coats, and shoes had helped the struggling, needy family. Her pocket money had often bought bread, beans, milk, and oranges for them.

In a few minutes Annette had returned.

"They'll answer," she whispered. "I'm to get their answer on the way to work in the morning. They said to give you this," and Annette laid a small copy of Steps to Christ in her hands.

The next day a letter came from Jack Lutes. The whole school was in the midst of the excitement of examinations, packing for vacation, and practicing for graduation. Rosalee was valedictorian and knew her part perfectly. But even so, she almost knew the letter by heart before night. Sweet phrases from it lingered in her mind.

```
       "Was   wonderful   meeting   you...   have   prayed...
God's hand... want His leading in my life... leaving
for Capital City next week.... Write again.... Pray
for me.

       "Your friend,
        "JACK LUTES."
```

Nothing forward, or presumptuous, but it was a friendly, kind, and understanding letter, which soothed her heart. Yet there was something, not in words, more indefinable, which made her hope for—she knew not what.

She answered the letter, and received another. Notes flew back and forth between her and the Lutes family by Annette. On graduation eve the neat copy of *The Desire of Ages*, sent by Jack, and the beautiful reference Bible from the Lutes family meant more than the diamond wrist watch her father and mother brought to her.

At home her heart could not seem to fit in with the life that went on there. The great rooms were lovely, perfectly appointed, and the machinery of the home went like clockwork. Yet she did not feel at home.

I can depend on Mrs. Merchant for everything!" her mother declared languidly one morning after a delightfully appetizing breakfast. "She manages menus, luncheons, table decorations, everything, and leaves me to be the 'grand lady.' What! no bacon, dear?" she addressed Rosalee. "What's the matter? You've always liked bacon fried to a crisp, with soft eggs. No coffee, either? What's happening?"

Rosalee looked up and saw her father's bushy brows drawn together, and his sharp eyes filled with suspicion. They seemed to be boring holes in her tender flesh.

I just fancy my eggs plain now," she answered simply, not wishing to start an argument, "and I've always liked cocoa," she added defensively. The matter was dropped there. But just before they left the table, her father spoke.

"Oh, I forgot to tell you, Rosalee. You're to teach in the summer school. The classes matriculate tomorrow.

School begins Monday." With that they all left the table, to the great relief of the bishop's daughter.

Then Rosalee began to plan. "I can save almost all my salary," she thought. "That is, excepting the tithe. I must plan ahead. No telling what father may do if he learns that I am determined to join the Adventist Church. He may even drive me away from home. He's like a madman when he's angry. There's no reasoning with him."

She was successful in her teaching, and the day pupils loved her. Her father kept close check on her work, and what he learned made his pompous old heart proud indeed. He decided to say nothing about her dietary fancies. That would die a natural death if he watched that she didn't get in touch with those friends. So the mail was sorted on the Reverend Hammond's desk every day.

But Rosalee had already thought of that, and had hired a private box, general delivery, at the post office. Her letters, closely hidden now, continued to be the greatest source of joy in her life. Her first month's salary was one hundred dollars.

"There! Get your own clothes now. Make the most of it!" laughed her father indulgently, as he counted it out in her hand. "You're off my hands now! If you were Jessica, that wouldn't go far."

Slowly she went to her room. Ten dollars for tithe. Ten dollars for offerings. She was sitting at her desk, starting a little budget book of her expenditures. In her neat square writing she had already written:

> Salary, July 1 .... $ 100.00
> Tithe 10.00
> Offerings 10.00

She heard a step behind her. Looking up, her heart plunged as she saw her father towering over her, his face black and contorted with rage.

"What's this?" he choked, reaching out and snatching her budget book.

"Tithe," he read scathingly. "Offerings," he sneered. "Well, you *won't!* No daughter of mine is going to play me tricks like this! You can just learn to do without money until you have some sense. You're the silliest little fool I have ever seen. Do you want to ruin my name and reputation?" With that he deliberately picked up her money, counted it, and put it into his pocket.

"Father," protested Rosalee, aghast at the look on his face. She thought for a moment he would strike her. "Father, I'm ashamed to remind you of this…it seems so ungrateful…but I was twenty-one years old in January."

"Yes, and you act as if you're twenty-one months old!" he answered hotly. "Jessica's baby is a genius compared with you. Why, I'll have you committed to an insane asylum before I let you spoil my name!"

"Well, then, I'll leave, Father!" she answered sadly. "You leave me no alternative. I can't stay here."

"Not much you don't, miss!" he shouted angrily. "Every thread you have on belongs to me. You don't leave this house until you are in your right mind!"

With that he left the room, stamping along the halls angrily. He banged the door to his own room hard, and Rosalee thought she heard something fall down and crash.

She rose and looked around the room with a sense of frustration. Was ever a girl placed in such a dreadful position? A prisoner in her own home! Forbidden to follow her own conscience! She'd have to leave. She'd have to. She'd send money home to pay for the clothing she wore away. She wouldn't be taunted and dictated to, and bullied.

She got a week-end case out of the wardrobe and began to pack it hastily. She would take only the simplest of necessities, for she must hurry. He'd come back in a few minutes. The train would leave at five.

In her purse was a graduation check from Grandma Snell, enough to keep her for several weeks. The Lutes! Dare she go there? Where else could she go? Going to the window, she dropped the case down to the petunia bed below.

Turning to her desk, she wrote a brief note, and weighted it down with the ink bottle, so it wouldn't blow away.

> "DEAR DADDY AND MOTHER,
>
> "I'm sorry, but I have to go. Things are too difficult for me. I must serve my God as I believe. I will write to you and send you the money for the clothing I am wearing and taking. I love you both. I want to do right more than anything on earth.
>
> "ROSALEE."

In ten minutes Rosalee was in the station. She'd gone past the post office and found two letters. One from Jack, and one from the Lutes family. The train was in the station. She was just in time.

When she was comfortably settled, with her little case in the rack overhead, she opened her handbag and took out the two letters. Perhaps if she read them, they would quiet her tensed nerves. Tears stung her eyelids. She was trembling from head to foot. It hurts to be uprooted. Old roots go deep. It hurts to be shouted at and ordered around, especially when a person is doing the best he knows how to do; especially when one is striving for a perfect life. Then suddenly a text Mrs. Lutes frequently quoted came into her mind.

"Great peace have they which love thy law: and nothing shall offend them."

She sat pondering the text—not seeing the kaleidoscope of farms and rivers and valleys that swept past the car windows. "Give *me* that peace, dear Lord," she prayed. "I love thy law—oh, yes, I love it! " Then with steady fingers she tore open her letter from Jack, and settled herself to enjoy it.

He told of the great city effort, of the crowds and crowds of people, of the contacts he had already made with interested people.

"Oh, it's a great life, this, working for the Lord, and feeling oneself a part of a worldwide soul-winning movement! I wish you were here. We need a pianist badly. The church women are helping us, but none of them can play very well for congregational singing, though they are eager to help. The evangelist told me to scout for one, and I thought of you right away. You'd board with Evangelist Coyne's family. Think about it, and let me know."

She sat for a long time with the open letter in her lap. Before she left her home, she had knelt briefly by her bed and prayed for the Lord to open the way so that she could "follow on to know the Lord." Now, this had come an opportunity already to serve the Jesus she had learned to love. God had begun to answer her prayer.

Dusk was falling when the train stopped at the small, familiar college town where she had gone to school. Rosalee was the only one to get off. Swiftly she made her way, like a homing pigeon, to the place where she knew love, sympathy, and goodness dwelt. Her heart seemed to run ahead of her as she hurried up the sloping sidewalk toward the house on the hill. She must watch her step; no need to hurry today and risk skinned knees and torn stockings. She smiled wanly there in the half light. Wasn't a broken heart harder to mend than skinned knees?

The welcome Rosalee received was just as cordial as she had known it would be. Mrs. Lutes and Barbara kissed her. Johnny ran and got her a glass of cold milk, spilling a little on the way back, but believing as small boys do that food cures most of the ills of the world. Mr. Lutes, with characteristic thoughtfulness, took her bag and coat and hat to the guest room. Then they gathered around her to hear her story.

"Tell us all about it, dearie," said Mrs. Lutes, in her warm, motherly voice. "It will do your heart good to air all your troubles."

They sat around her and listened, weeping as she wept, yet rejoicing that her faith had never wavered, even though it meant severing the dearest ties on earth.

"You mustn't let your mother and father worry, dear," said Mrs. Lutes. "We must get them word someway that you're all right."

Then Rosalee read Jack's letter to them. They were speechless for a few moments.

"Why, that seems like an opening from the Lord," Jim Lutes commented thoughtfully. "But we must not run before Him. We must wait patiently for His word in this matter. Let us pray."

Reverently they all knelt around Rosalee. Mr. Lutes prayed in his strong voice for guidance and wisdom. Mrs. Lutes prayed for peace and serenity and reconciliation.

"A true and a good woman," thought Rosalee. "Ready to pour oil and wine on the bleeding wounds of this world! "

Even Bobby and Barbara prayed—sweet, childish prayers, that everything would "be all right." Childish fingers reaching instinctively for a security that call only be found in Christ Jesus!

Praying, as such, was a new and beautiful experience to Rosalee. As a bishop's daughter, she had *learned to say* prayers. "Now I lay me" and "Loving Jesus, meek and mild," and, of course, the Lord's prayer had been repeated many times, but with little thought. But this praying, this opening of the heart to God as to a loved and trusted friend, was quite a new thing. Yes, Rosalee prayed because she wanted to; she prayed and wept there in that loving circle with Jesus and trusted friends. It seemed that she could see His dear face, His loving eyes clouded with sympathy, His wounded hands raised to bless her.

When they rose, Mr. Lutes spoke first.

"I have a feeling that you should go," he said. "But let us test the Lord. If the telephone should ring in the next ten minutes, for any reason whatsoever, let us phone the station and find out when the next train goes to Capital City."

Rosalee was amazed at his absolute trust in God's guidance. "God can make someone call us, if He wants you to go," he said confidently.

"But if it doesn't ring?" she asked fearfully.

"Then we'll just trust that God wants us to wait," he answered simply.

But even as he finished that very sentence, as if the telephone had been eavesdropping and conniving, the bell rang shrilly. They all jumped.

"Hello! Hello!" Mr. Lutes was speaking.

"Capital City calling," he turned and spoke to those listening. "Isn't this a coincidence?"

"Hello, Jack? Why, yes. *She's here*. Never mind why or how; it's a long story! Yes, you can talk to her." And with that he handed the receiver to Rosalee.

"Hello, Jack."

"Yes, oh, yes."

"Yes, I can come. We just prayed."

"On the next train."

"At nine? Oh, I must hurry then."

"Be seeing you."

"Bye."

Her cheeks were very, very red and her eyes shone like stars when she turned from the telephone.

"God *did* answer, as you said," she cried. "Why It seems almost too wonderful to believe!"

" 'Prayer is the key in the hand of faith to unlock heaven's storehouse, where are treasured the boundless resources of Omnipotence,'" quoted Mrs. Lutes.

"I'll get out the car," called -,Mr. Lutes from the kitchen. "Let's all take her. Wrap the baby in a blanket. This is an extraordinary occasion calling for 'all hands' to be present."

At the station Mr. Lutes saw to the getting of Rosalee's ticket. Fortunately, she got a sleeper. She stood on the platform of the moving train and waved at them until they were out of sight. Then, because she knew she was going to cry, and cry, and cry, she was glad that the porter had made up her bed.

Her tears were not tears of sorrow, but such as a lost child might shed when he has been found and cradled again in his mother's arms. She found comfort in the everlasting arms. She sobbed into her pillow for a long tune, then fell into such a restful sleep that she barely wakened in time to dress before the train pulled into Capital City.

She saw Jack before she went down the steps, tall, smiling, waving, and pressing through the crowd to greet her. Strange-she'd seen him only once, but through his letters he seemed like an old friend.

"Rosalee!

"Jack! "

105

"God is good, isn't He?"

"He is, indeed, Jack. I'm learning to trust Him more every day."

They were walking up the inclined plane to the gates, each more eager to hear the other's voice than to talk. In the parking lot beyond, Jack led her to his car.

"Isn't she a beauty?" he said, opening the door of the shining sedan. "Dad and Jim helped me with the down payment. Have to have a car in my work," he added. "So many people call for Bible studies every day."

"Oh, I wish I could help. But I haven't even been baptized myself yet! I *want* to be as soon as I learn enough."

"I've thought of that, and I asked Pastor Coyne. He thinks that if you would go with one of the Bible instructors every day as she pays her calls, you would be instructed in no time, and would soon be eligible for baptism. Well, here we are at Pastor Coyne's. We're just in time for breakfast. They asked me to eat with them this morning, so you wouldn't feel so strange."

The door opened before they were up the steps of the big, homey two-story house. Pastor and Mrs. Coyne were coming eagerly to meet them. "So this is the girl who plays so well, whom Jack has been talking about so enthusiastically. He says you're learning this blessed truth too! God bless you, my dear," greeted Mr. Coyne.

Rosalee noted his deep, beautiful voice, the strong, kind face, the firm clasp of his hand, and the burning brown eyes beneath bushy brows.

Then Mrs. Coyne took her hand.

"Welcome, dear," she said sweetly. "You're hungry, and breakfast will spoil if we don't eat it right away. I'm all ready to make the toast and bake the omelet. Here is your room, dear. It belonged to our daughter, Marjorie. She is married now and is living in Texas."

Before Rosalee had quite finished washing in the big blue and cream bathroom, the bell tinkled downstairs, and she was ushered into the simple hominess of a gay breakfast nook. Everything had a familiar air—as if she had been there before. "Why—why!" she thought excitedly, its like the Lutes home. It's because-God fives here too. That *must* be it!"

Gay, cheerful talk went back and forth. Friendly banter too, but not coarse or in bad taste. Everyone seemed happy.

"How about your getting familiar with your work, Miss Rosalee?" asked the pastor after breakfast. "My wife and Jack will show you the songs we sing, and you can plan the music for tonight this morning. This afternoon you rest."

"Oh! am I to start right away?"

"Oh, surely, we need you very much, and Jack led us to believe you need us too. Jack is a musician too, and maybe you can plan some things together."

The songbooks—*Solos and Duets,* by Rodeheaver, *Gospel in Song, Church Hymnal*, and a dozen others of different titles—were laid out.

It was a wonderful morning. Mrs. Coyne sat and knitted on a tiny pink sweater, "for my granddaughter," she had told Rosalee proudly, and showed her pictures of a rosy, smiling baby.

Rosalee played and Jack sang. Then he suggested that she sing while he played. Then Mrs. Coyne played for them to sing duets. "I used to teach music, but daddy needs me as a receptionist," she explained. "I'll be glad to play when you two sing duets. By the way, Miss Rosalee—"

"Rosalee to *you*, please," smiled the girl happily.

"Well, then, Rosalee, can you by chance play the pipe organ? We have not been able to use the pipe organ in the hall, since none of us knows enough about it to produce a note.

"Lead me to it," laughed Rosalee. "I've had five years of pipe organ right along with my piano lessons. I could play one in the dark!"

"Then we arc very fortunate, dear," said Mrs. Coyne. Her bright eyes wandered to the mantle clock. "My, oh, me!" she exclaimed. "Is that clock right? Daddy will be home in ten minutes, and dinner is not even started!"

"Let us help you!" cried Jack, seizing Rosalee's hand, and they all hurried to the kitchen together. There was a great deal of fun and laughter and commotion in the next ten minutes, but a lot of work was done too, for when Pastor Coyne opened the front door at high noon, tempting and delightful odors assailed his nostrils. Wonderful things can be done these days in a remarkably short time, thanks to frozen foods, pressure cookers, ready mixes, and can openers!

When Bishop Hammond stamped out of Rosalee's room, he thought that he could never be any angrier. Opposition always incensed him, but plain, unadulterated insubordination fairly drove him mad.

How could he hold up his head if one of his own children went off on such a silly tangent?

But the thing that angered him most was that he realized only too well the futility of trying to prove his assertions. He had tried that disastrously once with these law-observing, text-quoting Adventist preachers, and had hardly got away with a whole hide. Their laity were better informed on Scripture than most of the parsons sent out from the seminaries these days. To clash with any one of them meant a singeing. The best course was to steer Rosalee clear by force, send her off to Grandma Snell's or on a sea voyage, or some other place, he knew not where.

No—no—he couldn't send her to granny's; there was a large Adventist church and school in that very town. He couldn't send her on a voyage, for they say there are missionaries from that sect on nearly every boat that sails the seas. It would be best to keep her here and change her mind by force. She had always been putty in his hands before.

By the time he got to his study he had decided to confer with a minister friend who lived in another part of the town; so he got out the car and drove directly there. Rosalee's mother was attending a bridge party, and it was easy for him to slip away.

It was dark by the time he got home from a most unsatisfactory interview. The house was dark except for a light in the kitchen and the dining room, where the servants were working. Where was Rosalee? In her room pouting, he supposed. Well, let her pout. He'd show her. Yet, had he known it, at this very moment she was being warmly welcomed in the Lutes home.

Fortunately for them all, he didn't know, or he'd have driven fiercely there to try to take his rebellious daughter home by force.

Calling, turning on lights, peering, prowling, he did not find her. He didn't expect, hence didn't see, the little tear-stained note. Then he decided with relief that she'd probably gone over to Jessica's. That would be a good thing. Jessica would laugh the foolishness out of her. But even as these thoughts crossed his mind, he felt a pang of conscience. He knew in his heart of hearts that he didn't want his little ewe lamb to be like Jessica—Jessica, who could become intoxicated and brazen it out, laughing and blowing smoke rings right in his face. Jessica, whose babies hardly knew her, what with the dances, night clubs, and parties claiming nearly every moment of her time.

"No," he spoke aloud, heavily, "no, I don't want her to be like Jessica. Not like Jessica. Oh, no."

Then the dinner bell rang. He arose and went in to a lonely meal. Where *was* Rosalee?

"Madame called while you were gone," said the maid. "She said for you to go ahead and eat dinner without her. She is unavoidably detained at the Haughton-Smith's."

"Is this home?" he asked himself wearily. What was it Rosy said that last night she talked to him at the college? "That is not the way a home should be run. There ought to be love and family life there. The children should know and love their father and mother," Rosalee had said. Yet Rosalee had never known such a life! How did she find out about things like that? He remembered that Clara was proud to display the little girls in their silk frocks, ribbons, and curls, but responsibility flowed from her like water from a duck's back. If anything unpleasant occurred, like a skinned knee, a streaming nose, or a torn frock, she would always say, "There, there, run now to Mary to fix you up. You will get mother all dirty and messy.

Handsomely gowned and attractively coifed, she loved the role of "mother" if there was no unpleasantness or inconvenience linked with it.

Jotham sat there in the candlelit room and thought of his own boyhood back in Iowa, and he knew that this spacious, perfectly appointed show place was not a home.

He remembered his mother's last visit with them before she died. Clara had pouted for days after she left.

"Coming in and upsetting a well-ordered household like that," she had fumed again and again, until Jotham had hated the phrase.

His mother had died not long after that, and for a long time he couldn't step into his spacious tile and chromium kitchen without seeing her there teaching Jessica and Rosalee to make cookies, much to Clara's discomfiture.

"Why, Grandma, I never had so much fun before," Jessica had declared, putting her own production, a sheet of cookies—little scalloped discs of spicy sweetness—into the oven.

Rosalee had flour on her happy little face and was rolling her own cookies with a bottle.

"Isn't this fun, Daddy? And granny says gardens are fun too—pulling up little yellow carrots is like finding little gold wedges in the morning. Daddy, why can't we have a garden?"

Then he remembered the three, like pirate conspirators, bending and inspecting the baking cookies through the glass of the oven door.

"Now, I call that wonderful, girls," his mother had said warmly. "Electricity and all that. But Jotham, that big woodstove, with the full woodbox, out on the farm, the linoleum on the floor and the oilcloth on the table, were the height of elegance to me. I could get a fine meal with those conveniences. Remember, suppertime was the best, when there wasn't any hurry or scurry. Poppie coming in from doing the chores; you and Sam and Betsy, God love her, washing your little faces and hands at the wash bench by the pitcher pump."

"Remember the roller towel, Mamma?" he had asked.

"Oh, yes, Jotham. I found one of those old towels in one of the trunks last week, and I cried my eyes out over it. Why, I don't know, unless I was crying over something that's a rare thing these days. But I didn't know it then."

Jotham looked down at his beautifully served meal in distaste. "Yes, Mother," he thought, "you were right. It's a rare thing these days."

His little girls had never lacked for dolls, buggies, tricycles, and hobbyhorses. Yet they would gladly have left those purchased means of pleasure for a corked bottle, a floured board, grandma, and a lump of dough. Why? Jotham knew. Yet he had built his life as he had wanted it. He had thought he hadn't liked chores and farmwork and the smell of cows at milking time. Yet now he knew that, though he'd achieved what he fondly termed his "goal in life," he had paid a fearful price. It was nine o'clock when he arose from the table, the exact time Rosalee was boarding the train for Capital City.

He went back to the living room. Then, restlessly, he went to the study. Not being able to content himself there, he wandered down the hall to Rosy's room. Then he saw the note. When he had finished reading it, the tears were streaming down his sagging old cheeks. He sat down heavily and covered his face with his hands.

"O Rosy, Rosy, what have I done to you? What have I done? Mother, Mother, tell me what to do about Rosy. *You* always knew. *You* always helped me, Mamma."

Though the strong, comforting voice had been stilled these many years, and the busy hands he had loved so much had turned to dust, yet he knew what she would say. He could almost bear her sure, persuasive tones.

"Now, Jotham, she's stubborn like you. She can't be forced. You have to lead her, Jotham. None of the Hammonds would be driven. Just wasn't their nature. Just you coax her, love her, and edge things on gentlelike. All of us oldsters get to thinking children aren't human beings. You have to get close to children or you'll lose them for good. Now, if she's done something wrong—"

"But, Mamma," she *hasn't*."

Then he caught himself up, realizing that in this funny, imaginary conversation he had made an admission he hand not wanted to make. Yet he knew in his heart that his mother had been something of a religious renegade herself. After he had become a bishop, she had spoken to him about infant baptism one day.

"According to my way of thinking, Jotham, it isn't reasonable, sprinkling water on those babies. What do they know or care about sanctification, justification, election, and predestination? Now, if they'd take them down to the Susquehanna and duck them in, as the Bible teaches, all they'd get would be an extra bath that day. Baptism, according to my thinking, just ought to be for people who have decided to change their way of living and do differently.

Those babies aren't going to change. They'll spit up milk, get colic, and cry all night, just as before."

Then she had made a big to-do about Easter once, he remembered. "Pure sickening," she had said. "People who don't give a hoot about religion or God or living right, promenading and prancing to church on Easter, just to show off fine apparel. Fine clothes don't make fine ladies, I always say. Tear off that fancy attire, and what do you have? An ugly, base character.

"Yes, Mamma, yes. You were right. But what about Rosalee?"

Again he could imagine that sweet, firm answer.

"Don't crowd her, Jotham. And don't ever punish her for something that isn't wrong. Has Rosy done wrong? Ask God about this, Jotham. That's your job, you know."

"All right, Mamma. I'll do as you tell me. I'll ask God. But Rosy hasn't done wrong, Mamma. She's like you, she won't take anyone's word for anything, but thinks things out herself. Someway now, Mamma, I'm glad she's like you!"

Then stumbling, half blinded by his tears, he went to his study and fell to his knees, and prayed incoherently for a long time.

Yet even while he knelt there, sobbing, trembling, yet not daring to ask for anything, fearing that God might pour the vials of His wrath upon him, Rosalee was snuggled sound asleep in the Pullman berth, and the train, whistling shrilly, was racing down the track, bearing Jotham's little ewe lamb to a higher, better, and more beautiful life.

* * * * *

The big hall where the evangelistic effort was being held was softly lighted. "Sister" McLeod and "Sister" Parker, as they had been introduced to Rosalee, were arranging the flowers they had brought in from their ample country gardens.

"These crimson ramblers are from a start my papa fetched over from Scotland," Sister McLeod had told her proudly as she arranged the lovely bright flowers and ferns in vases. "They draw a prize every year at the fair."

A should think they would," agreed Rosalee. "They're gorgeous. Yours are lovely too," she told gentle little Mrs. Parker, who had her vases arranged tastefully also.

"I'm glad you like them," she said shyly. "These were Virgie's favorites. She was my daughter. She died last year."

"Oh, they are lovely," Rosalee whispered, "and I'm sorry about Virgie. You must be very lonely."

Tears stood in the woman's eyes.

"You're a good girl, dearie. I'm glad you came."

Every heart has its own sorrow, grief, and trouble, Rosalee thought as she hastened up the rostrum steps. Jack was beckoning to her.

"Time for you to begin the organ," he whispered. "Here's your book. I picked up the one you asked me to get at Strand's. Good luck—God bless you."

As she mounted the choir loft the great organ stood before her, opened invitingly. Four manuals, she noted gladly. Sitting down, she glanced up briefly and saw the youthful faces of the choir members upon her, watching with friendly, interested eyes. Tonight, after the services, she and Jack would practice with them. She'd just have to follow tonight. Then she turned to the organ, and its rich music filled the hall. Through the mirror she saw the great auditorium filling with people. They came in groups rather than filtering in one by one. This was wonderful.

The whole service was magnificent. Rosalee realized that it was the first Adventist sermon she had ever heard.

In Harrington Heights there was no church, and she had tried in her own way to keep Sabbath at home.

The evangelist had given an excellent talk on the saints' inheritance. Someway, as he painted gorgeous word pictures of the beautiful land where sorrow will never come, where there will be no death, pain, or misery, Rosalee felt as if she could weep and shout for joy at the same time. Then as this servant of God built up to the grandeur and glory and beauty of that goodly land, Rosalee thought she couldn't stand it—it was all so wonderful. She bit her lip to keep it from trembling.

Jack had seated himself at the piano, and the choir watched his every movement as they waited for his signal.

"For behold, I create new heavens, and a new earth," read the speaker in a voice of great gladness. "And the former shall not be remembered, nor come into mind."

Instantly the choir responded like a marvelous echo:

> "We speak of the realms of the blest,
>   That country so bright and so fair,
>   And oft are its glories confessed—
>   But what must it be to be there!"

112

"The wilderness and the solitary place shall be glad for them; and the desert shall rejoice, and blossom as the rose," continued the evangelist in a voice filled with joy, and triumph, and exultation. "It shall blossom abundantly, and rejoice even with joy and singing: the glory of Lebanon shall be given unto it, the excellency of Carmel and Sharon, they shall see the glory of the Lord, and the excellency of our God."

The choir instantly answered:

> "We speak of its pathway of gold—
> Its walls decked with jewels so rare,
> Its wonders and pleasures untold—
> But what must it be to be there!"

Again the fine voice of the man of God:

"The eyes of the blind shall be opened, and the ears of the deaf shall be unstopped. Then shall the lame man leap as an hart, and the tongue of the dumb sing: for in the wilderness shall waters break out, and streams in the desert."

The sweet singers answered with:

> "Do thou, midst temptation and woe,
> For heaven my spirit prepare;
> And shortly I also shall know
> And feel what it is to be there."

"Therefore," continued the evangelist, "the redeemed of the Lord shall return, and come with singing unto Zion; and everlasting joy shall be upon their head: they shall obtain gladness and joy; and sorrow and mourning shall flee away."

"Every valley shall be exalted, and every mountain and hill shall be made low:…and the glory of the Lord shall be revealed…: for the mouth of the Lord bath spoken it."

As a grand finale the choir sang:

> "Then o'er the bright fields we shall roam,
> In glory celestial and fair,
> With saints and with angels at home,
> And *Jesus Himself* will be there."

The effect was wonderful. All over that vast audience people were quietly weeping.

Now she knew why Jack had asked her to play that arrangement from Handel's oratorio *The Messiah* to close— "Every valley shall be exalted." The organ seemed to speak the words to her full heart as they poured forth from the mighty golden pipes hidden in the misty darkness above. She could see the caped usherettes, Mrs. Coyne, cordial and dignified, and Pastor Coyne, kind and sincere, at the door. They seemed to be greeting everyone, so happily, so personally. That must be a gift straight from God. She must watch them closely and maybe she might have a portion of their blessed spirit. Heaven was very near that night. And as is characteristic of those who find Jesus infinitely precious, she wanted to share Him with those she loved.

So that night, before she went to bed, she wrote a long letter to her mother and father. She tried to make the letter gracious and loving, with no trace of bitterness at the harsh treatment she had received. She left out the bitterness and the blame, which a smaller soul might have included. Her pen flew, for her soul was still aglow with a consciousness of what the Lord is preparing for those who love Him, which she had heard in such a wonderful setting that evening.

The next morning Jack and she took the letter and went downtown to mail it. Pastor and Mrs. Coyne advised him to take her around town also.

There were a few little things she needed to buy too, which in her haste she hadn't brought along.

So he showed her where the stationery and bookstore was, and she bought envelopes, paper, and ink. They went all through the dime stores, and saw many interesting things. It was so much fun walking with Jack. He was an interesting companion, and his comical remarks kept her laughing. Then near dinnertime, when they realized they must hurry, he bought two large double-dip ice-cream cones, and they ate them in the car before they started.

"Just the commonest things are the most fun if you're with someone you like," thought Rosalee.

"She is so wholesome and gets fun out of everything," thought Jack.

It wasn't long until Rosalee was in the swing of everything, practicing, singing, selecting, and arranging all the morning. Then she was off with Miss Conners for a delightful afternoon of Bible study. Sometimes she would shyly put in a word or two, and Miss Conners always thanked her afterward. It gave her greater courage and made her feel as if she "belonged."

She hadn't been in Capital City quite a week when she and Jack sang a duet one evening. They had tried it several days before, and their voices harmonized so beautifully that Pastor Coyne asked them to sing it during an appeal he wanted to make at the end of this meeting.

"You see," he said, "this is an important evening. I present and summarize the final phases of the Sabbath, the perpetuity and the binding character of the law. I think this is Just the very song to touch hearts and lead them to make the right decision."

After a most tender appeal—an appeal that Rosalee thought must melt even hearts of stone, they arose quietly to sing:

"There's a line that is drawn by rejecting our Lord,
  Where the call of His Spirit is lost,
And you hurry along with the pleasure-mad throng,
  Have you counted, have you counted, the cost?"

Launching into the chorus, sensing the solemnity of the words and enjoying the harmony of their two voices, Rosalee let her eyes wander down over the great sea of faces upturned toward her. Suddenly her heart plunged and skipped a beat. She almost lost her place in the song, for *there*, seated on the very *first* row, looking straight into her eyes, was the Reverend Jotham Hammond! And greater than the wonder of seeing him there was her observation that the haughty, arrogant look was quite gone from his face. He had his big white handkerchief out, and was wiping the tears from his eyes!

After Jotham's session in the study he arose refreshed. He felt as if a great burden had been rolled away. But it was still going to be hard to adjust himself to a new order of things—a new way of thinking. Of course, he wasn't prepared to make any changes in his own life *yet*, or even to do any research that might be devastating, but he'd just *have* to let Rosy do as *she* pleased.

He remembered that when he was studying church history in the old seminary days, he read in Tertullian that the blood of the Christian martyrs was as seed. Tertullian had written up what one Christian said to a pagan ruler in protest against the horrible persecution he was instigating. It had so inspired Jotham then that he had underlined it. He must have been something like his old mother in those days. Stay! Where's that book? Here! and leafing through it rapidly he'd found the place he had underlined so long ago.

"You may fall us, torture us, condemn us—your injustice is a proof that we are innocent. Nor does your cruelty avail you. The more ye mow us down, the more quickly we grow; the blood of Christians is fresh seed."

Jotham knew that the more he opposed a girl like his Rosy, the more determined she would be. She was made of the stuff martyrs are made of, bless her.

Just then he heard the front door open, and he knew that Clara, his wife, had come home. He wished his heart would leap to meet her. He wished he could honestly say he was glad to see her and had missed her. But he hadn't, he thought guiltily. They had never been very near together, but in the years since their marriage they had drifted so far apart that it seemed as if they were strangers.

Long ago she had moved Jotham's bed into one of the guest chambers upstairs, so she would have room for a big desk for her "club work," she said, and Jotham had not cared in particular. Her supreme neglect of anything and everything except what contributed to her own pride, pleasure, or egotism had long since ceased to amaze him. There was only a dull ache when he stopped and thought of what might have been.

She was inordinately proud of saying, "My husband, Bishop Hammond," "our married daughter, Jessica" (then she would explain archly, "She married Eric Sneed-Selvers, the son of the big department store magnate. They have a lovely country home, and two adorable babies").

The door of his study opened, and Clara stood there.

"Ah, Jotham! not in bed?" she asked in her cold, cultured voice. "Where is Rosalee?"

"She's gone." He hadn't the courage to look up.

"Gone? Gone where?"

"I don't know,"

His wife sat down, her face cold with exasperation.

"Jotham, why do you persist in acting so aggravating. You seem to take delight in angering and discommoding me. Tell me where Rosalee is and stop this nonsense."

Jotham raised his face. He looked years older. "Clara, I tell you I don't know. This afternoon we had a quarrel. I caught her taking a tithe out of her money to pay into the Adventist Church. I became so angry that I almost hit her. You know, I told you that she was interested in that sect before she left college, and had laid down the law to her. Well, today I discovered she was still interested in their beliefs, and that the thing had grown till I saw it was going to take extreme measures to put a stop to it. Well, I took those measures, and this is the result. She's gone, and, Clara, she's gone for keeps. You can't force Rosalee into a mold. I've discovered that today."

Bleak surprise, mingled with disdain at first, flashed across his wife's florid face.

"O Jotham, how tiresome! The *Adventist* Church! Why, they're *queer*. I'll have to admit they're good people, but they don't believe in dancing, smoking, or even drinking *moderately*. Sophie Sellers says her best housemaid, Annie, is an Adventist, and won't even go into a roadhouse. She says that she won't consider going to the movies. What's got into Rosalee, anyway? Why can't she be like Jessica? "

"Clara, would you *want* her to be like Jessica?"

His wife's face sagged, and she looked away guiltily. Her lips trembled.

"No, I suppose I just said that automatically. But, Jotham, Eric came to me today and told me he was divorcing Jessica and asking for custody of the babies. He says that sometimes she spends two or three days at a time with that crowd. I've been hunting her today, Jotham. I'm wild with worry, and I found her this evening at the Flaming Flamingo with that horrible Dopey Thompson, who, they say, never draws a sober breath. I took her home, and if ever I talked straight to anyone, I did to Jessica. I made her some black coffee and got her sobered up, and Eric and I really read the riot act to her. I left her crying. I told Eric to bring her and the babies and come over here tomorrow. I thought if we could get her away from that wild crowd for a few weeks, and with Rosalee, we might help her. But, O Jotham, Rosy is gone now."

"Rosy is gone now, 11 repeated Jotham brokenly. "Clara, we've failed with our girls. They haven't any confidence in us.

"You know, Jotham," his wife answered seriously, "all the time I was shaking and rousing Jessica in that disgusting roadhouse. with the juke boxes blaring and the people snickering and the whole place in an uproar, I thought of how kind and good our Rosy is, staying at home, clean, calm, quiet, and sweet. I think we should have let her alone and not tried to force her will. She hasn't done any wrong.

"I know that now, and, Mother, I've been praying this evening, and I've someway been thinking of my mother.

She would have rejoiced in Rosalee if she had lived to see this day."

"I believe she would," his wife answered thoughtfully.

"You know, Jotham, your mother used to irritate me, for I knew she didn't approve of my shallow, silly life. One day, when I'd sent Rosalee and Jessica to the park with the maid, she looked at me queerly and said, 'You don't know what you're missing, Clara. You're bartering your young motherhood in the marketplace. There'll be no live coals of memory to warm by when you get old.' It angered me at the time, but I know she was right, and I knew it then, but I was too stubborn to heed her."

"If Rosy writes, Mother, what shall we do?" Jotham leaned forward and watched his wife's face closely. This was the first talk they had had together in many years. Even in his sorrow, Jotham was glad for this mournful shred of companionship. He had longed for it in vain for so long.

"Why, we must let her do as she believes," his wife answered. "Your mother was always saying that the ways of God are past finding out. There might be a lesson in Rosalee's experience for all of us."

The next day, Jessica, Eric, and the babies arrived, and a new Clara greeted them. She took one little girl in her arms and the other by the hand.

"Why, Mom!" drawled Jessica in mild surprise. "Gone domestic, huh?" She stopped at the door, opened her cigarette case, and started to take one out. Clara reached out and took the little golden box.

"No, Jessica," she said firmly. "Let's stop that too. No, don't get provoked now! Mother wants to help you. Let's all try together. I haven't been a good mother to you, and I've quit smoking too. This is the only way to save your home, dear. This is an emergency."

Jessica opened her mouth to say something, then closed it again. She loved her babies, and her husband too, and she realized that she would have to change, or her home would surely be spoiled. So, queerly enough, Jessica agreed in her mind to give her mother's way a trial.

"Let's go out and play with the children awhile," the mother suggested right at first, and the two went to the back yard. A little rubber wading pool had been inflated and filled with water. It wasn't long till the children, in wisps of suits, were shouting and laughing joyously.

It was a new experience to have mother and grandmother around. It meant so much more to little hearts than the companionship of any hired help.

"Fun, Mommy, fun!" shouted little Karen. The baby, Sally Jo, sat in the water spattering it liberally, laughing in sucking little gasps that were adorable. Eric wandered out and sat down nearby.

"Jessica," he said, "this quiet back yard, with mother and the babies, is more fun than anything else, isn't it? The dappled shade, the close-clipped grass, the laughing babies—and you."

"Yes, Eric, I agree." And Jessica put down the tall glass from which she was drinking ice water. "I agree, and even though I'm on needles and pins right now for a drink and a smoke, I'm not going to take either. Perhaps it won't be so bad tomorrow."

Jotham came out just then. He smiled at the quiet little group in the shade.

"Listen, you all," he put in. "Ah, here's grandpa's darling," he turned to say to Karen when she ran gleefully to him, her little wet face glowing.

"Why don't you go up to our cabin for a vacation? It's all alone up there by the lake. And, Jessica, you just can't drink or smoke there if there is no smoke or drink. And none of the crowd can find you till you're stronger. They've kept the line hot all morning. Seems as if I've done nothing but answer the phone and say, 'No, she's not available now. I'm very sorry.' Mother will go with you. I'd go, but I want to stay around and see whether any word comes from Rosy. My heart is full of my other poor little girl too."

So the next afternoon Eric and Jessica, Clara and the babies, went away in the station wagon for a restful vacation from the steaming city. Mrs. Merchant sat in the back, her spine as straight as a ramrod, her busy domestic mind already on the menus she would prepare on the bottled gas stove up there at the cabin, with all the supplies she had brought along. Clara knew that she would think of everything, so she hadn't bothered her head about culinary details. She had been rudely awakened from her complacency by the crisis in Jessica's life and by Rosalee's disappearance. She was not the silly, spoiled woman at heart that she seemed to be, but flattery, plenty of money, love of display, and pride had worn a groove in her day-by-day existence from which she had found it hard to extricate herself. Just when she and Jotham seemed to be at the height of opulence and complacency, the blow had fallen. Perhaps God willed that it should be so. And, strangely enough, the crises in the lives of their daughters were as opposite as the poles. Yet each crisis must be met in its own way.

The second day after they had left, Jotham received Rosalee's long letter. He had heard the postman's ring and had gone tremblingly to the door. There, lying in the box was the letter addressed to him in Rosalee's square, neat handwriting. His hands shook so that he could hardly break the seal. Then when he did, he read the simple sweet letter through again and again. Several times he had had to take off his glasses and wipe the tears from his eyes. Rosalee! his baby! Pianist at a great evangelistic meeting. In spite of himself he felt an uplift of pride that this should be so. He had asked an old retired teacher to take Rosalee's place in the school, giving the lame excuse that the girl had needed a "rest."

The first thing he did was to telephone long distance to tell Clara. It would lift a great weight from her heart. Someway this newly found companionship between him and Clara was infinitely sweet. Before, she had seemed like a haughty, exacting stranger. Now she seemed like a necessary, beloved friend. There was all the difference in the world.

"Hello! hello! is that you, Clara?"

"Cool up there? You swim a lot?"

119

"Yes, hot here. I wish I could come, but I just got a letter from Rosalee."

"Yes, she's all right. She's playing the piano for a big evangelistic effort in Capital City."

"I was too, but I'm relieved. She seemed very happy. Her letter is as eloquent as a sermon. I'm sending it on to you, dear."

"What did you say?...Oh! You think I should?...Then I'll start now. I'll get there by seven tonight. Yes, I'll let you know. How's Jessica?"

"Well, I will praise the Lord if things turn out better. Bye, dear. Be seeing you!"

Jotham went directly to his room and packed a bag. Then he closed and locked the whole house. He backed his car out of the garage, and was soon on his way to Capital City—to see Rosalee.

As soon as the meeting was over, Rosalee went to the pipe organ to play while the people were going out. She wondered what her father would do and say. She was not in the least afraid or ashamed, for she had tried to act honorably in every way. So while her nimble fingers and feet were making the sweet "Godspeed" music that filled the hall like a benediction, she was praying to the all-wise God to guide her in what she did and said. She had had just a whispered word with Jack before she began to play.

"O Jack! Father's here!"

"He is! How did you know?"

"I saw him. Tell Pastor Coyne."

"I will. I'll tell him right now. Don't worry. Pastor will treat him like a Christian gentleman!"

"Of course! I know that! I trust him! "

"Well, bye, Rosalee. Don't you worry. We'll fix things! "

"I'm sure you will. Bye."

At last there was just a small group by the door, so the girl stopped playing and closed the organ. Jack was waiting for her by the choir steps.

I met your father, Rosalee," he whispered. "Come on, quick. He say's he's been sick with worry over you. The Coynes have invited him to their house. They asked me to come too."

"Did he act angry?" the girl whispered as they went down the long aisle. "You know, I told you how furious he was with me the day I left."

Jack laughed softly.

"O Rosalee! Pastor Coyne is really stupendous! When your father came up and introduced himself in a rather pompous manner, Pastor Coyne seized his hand as if he were a long-lost friend, and began to tell him how wonderful you are! "

"Oh, no!" protested Rosalee, giggling nervously.

"But oh, *yes!* my dear," Jack countered softly, "and that's adding *my* incontrovertible opinion too," he added, taking her hand in the half darkness. "We're almost there, but I have time to tell you just a little more. You could just see the ice melt in your father's eyes as the pastor laid on the praises—but sh! here we are!"

The next instant Rosalee was in her father's arms, and weeping for joy on his shoulder.

"O Daddy, Daddy, Daddy!" she cried, burrowing her head in his big shoulder.

"Rosy, baby, can you ever forgive daddy?" The pompous Jotham Hammond was openly weeping,

"'Course, Daddy, you just didn't understand how much it means to me to do just what I believe." Rosalee lifted an April face, wreathed in the sweetest smiles Jotham had ever seen. He kissed her unashamedly, all the professional austerity gone out of him.

In a few minutes the cavalcade of cars was on its way to the pastor's home. Pastor Coyne and his wife led the way, Rosalee and her father came next, and Jack, not to he outdone, brought up the rear.

It was only ten o'clock when they reached the roomy, comfortable house, and Mrs. Coyne hurried into the kitchen to make some cold orangeade, with directions that Rosalee show her father to the front guest room. In a few minutes they were all back in the living room, sipping the refreshing drink from the tall frosty glasses. Rosalee sat on the arm of her father's chair, and it was plain to everyone that Jotham's heart was wrapped up in the lovely girl. He could not keep from smiling, and as for Rosalee, her whole face was vibrant with joy.

"And who is *this* young man, pastor?" he asked, smiling at Jack.

"He is our song leader," replied the pastor. "In fact, it was through *him* that we got in touch with your daughter."

When Jotham looked puzzled, Rosalee began to tell him the whole story of how she found the Lutes family, and of the wonderful Bible studies they had had together. Her face glowed so, when she told of the happy home life she'd found there, that Jotham's heart smote him.

"I've cheated my babies," he told himself.

While she talked on and on, Jotham's eyes swept the group. Beautiful Mrs. Coyne was absorbed in the story, her knitting in her lap and her gentle face soft with sympathy. Pastor Coyne looked as serenely satisfied as one who hears a beloved truth corroborated. Then he glanced at Jack. In a second he knew the truth: this boy was in love with his Rosalee! Then he saw Rosalee's eyes turn to meet Jack's as the narrative reached the part he had played in her life. Ah! Jotham had seen that look before! And he recognized it, probably before even those most concerned had analyzed the depth and portent of their feeling for each other. That understanding look, that telegraphic message of pleasure in each other, was as old as the world itself. And he wasn't angry or displeased, no. After the lacquered-haired empty heads who had filled his house chasing after Jessica, this one seemed real. One knew in an instant that one could bank on his word and know that he would yield up his life before he would betray faith or love.

"So you see, Daddy," Rosalee turned the barrage of her soft-glowing eyes on Jotham's face, "you see, it doesn't seem as if it's all coincidence. Every part of my association with that family, every change they helped to make in my life, seemed to be ordered of God. I seemed to be swept away by a great tide of events that I had not directed at all. And, Daddy dear, I'm happy, so, so happy. And I want you to be happy too."

For a moment Jotham could not answer. He knew he could not say anything hateful or cross or even controversial, or he'd put out the soft light that seemed to glow like candles in his child's eyes.

"If you feel that God has led you, my darling," he said softly, tears running down his cheeks again, "I'll be the last one to stop you."

"O Daddy!" Rosalee's arms were about her father, and she was kissing his wet cheeks.

When she took him to his room that night, he told her briefly about their problem with Jessica and her family, and they both made a little pact to pray especially about that particular problem. It bound them closer than ever before.

"And I'll get Jack to pray too," Rosalee declared as she kissed him good night.

"Hah I" Jotham smiled covertly to himself as the door closed and he loosed his tie to take it off. "Hah! and the little darling doesn't even know she's been bitten!"

And he wasn't displeased.

No, not a bit.

Early the next morning Jotham and Pastor Coyne met in the living room for a little chat. Both men had arrived simultaneously at the bathroom door with shaving things, only to find it preoccupied by Rosalee or Mrs. Coyne at their early morning ablutions. By common consent they slipped into the living room to converse while they waited. Pastor Coyne laid his hand on Jotham's arm.

"You're going to be asked," he whispered, "to give that girl of yours away one of these days. Didn't you see what we all see?"

Jotham nodded understandingly.

Pastor Coyne continued. "And you mast not oppose this match. It is real love such as is seldom seen these days, and he's one of the finest young men it has ever been my good fortune to meet."

Jotham again nodded understandingly, his eyes dim with tears, and then they crept back to their bedrooms like two wily conspirators who recognized happiness when they saw it. It was wonderful.

*   *   *   *   *

The kitchen of the little white cottage was bright and sunny. A little table and a little cooky board and a big table and big cooky board were in active use. A tiny checked apron and a big checked apron were tied around two feminine waists.

"Mommie, this is fun!" little Jeanie smiled up into Mother Rosalee's happy face. "We's gettin' ready for daddy, isn't we?"

"Yes, darling, we are. And you can let him eat some of your cookies if you want to. He will like them."

"Ikem!" contributed Baby Jotham, like a little echo, from his play pen, holding out dimpled arms to anyone who would notice him.

"Oh! there's daddy now!" cried Rosalee. After washing her floury hands at the sink, she seized the baby, and she and Jeanie ran into the living room and right into Jack's outstretched arms as he opened the door.

"My darlings! My darlings!" Daddy Jack cried with deep joy in his voice and heart.

Kissing his wife and the rosy, happy babies, he realized with deep love and gratitude that a good wife and a happy home are indeed a foretaste of the glory and beauty of heaven.

And from this happy domestic scene of Jack and Rosalee Lutes in the homeland, we must hurry on to its sequel, a cutting from their later sacrificial service in the land Rosalee had so much dreaded to think about in her college days.

It was almost sunset, and Jack hadn't reached home yet. It had been almost three weeks since he had left for a long safari up into a territory where the Advent message had never been preached. But he had told Rosalee that he

Would be back on this very day, and he usually kept his promises,

Baby Jotham stood up in his crib, which Jack had made of wood sawed in a pit by African boys. Little Jean was making elaborate plans about daddy's return, which she was now confiding to a long-suffering tomcat, who had just permitted himself to be dressed in some doll clothes.

"Tomtat, our daddy is tummin, and we's gonna fits his baf. Nen we'll show him some letters from gampa and gamma. Nen he'll play thist a little ith Jofam 'n me. Nen we'll eat supper. Wanna eat supper, tomtat?"

"Yeow," contributed the feline hopefully.

"Da, Da, Da," remarked Jotham, conversationally.

Steps crunched on the gravel walk. Daddy? Rosalee ran to look. No, just the native boy who had come with milk from the *khola*. The sun was very low now, throwing into silhouette a whole row of African huts at the back of the mission.

Rosalee smiled when she thought of that night long ago at the Lutes house. She had been horrified at the thought of Africa and wild beasts, malaria and dysentery. "You wouldn't take Teeny to that awful place, would you?" she had asked incredulously. Yet here she was, a voluntary exile" as it were, on a remote and isolated station. Five years at training awkward black girls to sew, and cook, and keep house. Five years of listening to the gospel preached in a native tongue, and even singing beloved old gospel songs set to such strange tongue-twisting words.

Five years away from a ten-cent store, a supermarket, and an electric stove. Rosalee laughed aloud. "As if I care," she said to no one in particular. "I belong to the 4-J club—a charter member. Jesus—Jack—Jeanie—and—Jotham! "

"Did I hear my wife call my name?" asked a voice at the door. Jack stood there surveying, the peaceful scene before him, his heart in his eyes.

"Jack!" Rosalee leaped for the door.

"Daddy," cried Jeanie.

"Da, Da," babbled Jotham.

"Yeow," contributed tomcat, with a prolonged protesting howl.

We invite you to view the complete
selection of titles we publish at:

www.TEACHServices.com

Scan with your mobile
device to go directly
to our website.

Please write or email us your praises, reactions, or
thoughts about this or any other book we publish at:

TEACH Services, Inc.
P U B L I S H I N G

www.TEACHServices.com

P.O. Box 954
Ringgold, GA 30736

info@TEACHServices.com

TEACH Services, Inc., titles may be purchased in bulk for
educational, business, fund-raising, or sales promotional use.
For information, please e-mail:

BulkSales@TEACHServices.com

Finally, if you are interested in seeing
your own book in print, please contact us at

publishing@TEACHServices.com

We would be happy to review your manuscript for free.